BLUE
&
GOLD

A Bullying Memoir

By

Mary Powell, PhD, LCSW-R, NCPsyA

Table of Contents

Acknowledgments

My conquering the effects of bullying would not have been possible without the assistance of psychotherapists who treated me and professionals who trained me as well as others so dear to my heart. In particular, I thank my husband who stood behind me the entire time I simultaneously pursued my PhD and wrote this book.

I wish to thank all characters in this story, whether they had a positive or negative impact on me, for without them this would not have come to pass. I hold no grudges but want only the best for them.

Disclaimer

This book is a memoir. It reflects the author's present recollections of experiences over time. This book is written from my adolescent voice, not my adult one. I have attempted to recreate events and conversations from my memories of my experiences. In order to maintain anonymity, I have changed the names and, in some instances, identifying information of individuals such as physical properties, ethnicity, gender, and occupation. This story is told from the voice of an adolescent, and the narrative contains racism, sexism and heterosexism, as well as other material that might be offensive. This content does not reflect the viewpoints of the author today.

This book was not written to "get revenge" but rather to tell a story. Therapists have a past; that's why we are therapists. The author apologizes for any hurt feelings that may emerge as a result of this story and thanks the people portrayed. This memoir reflects only the years of 1988-1992 at this educational institution. The author claims no knowledge of any events that might have occurred in the school outside of the four years she attended. After her graduation, the author noticed via media that the institution became a place of academic and social excellence.

Contains mature content.

Foreword

I met Dr. Mary Powell in 2015 at an interview in my capacity as Senior Associate Dean when she was in her later stages of the PhD program at Fordham University Graduate School of Social Service. She was hoping to resume teaching as an adjunct. Upon reviewing her impressive Curriculum Vitae, I hired her to continue teaching the Master of Social Work (MSW) students in our program. A couple of years later, I became the new Chair of her dissertation. She and I connected well and therefore I believe I can offer a credible foreword to her book. I watched her grow as an adjunct professor and a doctoral student. She no longer struggles as a bullying victim but is now a leader, especially in her education of others.

Dr. Powell is also a psychotherapist in private practice. She has presented at several professional conferences on mindfulness, dialectical behavior therapy (DBT), clinician self-care, and how to implement these into the social work education curriculum. She wrote her dissertation on burnout, role ambiguity, and coping strategies among MSW students in field placement, which subsequently won the Reverend Dr. Langenfeld Award for the Most Outstanding PhD Dissertation. As the first researcher to find significant outcomes on the association of role ambiguity with burnout in MSW students, she is one of the most well-respected adjunct professors in our MSW program, primarily due to her efforts to enhance student well-being. Students have praised the efforts of Dr. Powell to help them find themselves in their professional journeys and have stated that her classes have helped them heal on a personal level. And so I am certain her patients have experienced similar outcomes.

Blue and Gold is a story that portrays a young Mary Powell who experienced emotional and verbal bullying at the hands of peers in an all-girls Catholic high school. The administration appeared to do little to stop the bullying. The journey is one of a desperate attempt to survive which shows the victim demonstrating both fight and flight tendencies. It is clear from the story that this teenager was suffering as a result, and her poor self-esteem is evident throughout. It not only depicts Mary's victimhood but moments of becoming an aggressor herself.

Bullying at the hands of her high school peers might very well have resulted from Mary's vulnerability. It is not uncommon for individuals who exhibit high vulnerability to become victims of abuse and bullying. But her victory results from her usage of inner resources and fierce determination. In her resolve, she found the middle ground between her heart and her aggression. From the bits and pieces of her shattered self-esteem, Mary created her unique personality.

Bullying is one of the most persistent types of hostility in schools and therefore has drawn a great deal of awareness in recent years. It is responsible for anxiety, depression, and even suicide in youth. Its alleviation involves the commitment of administration in schools to stop its occurrence. Introducing a human rights framework into bullying prevention work might alleviate practical problems interfering with its alleviation (Greene, 2006). Recovery from bullying may be achieved through insight-oriented therapy in which the patient re-experiences trauma along with more concrete treatments such as DBT.

This book is relevant to any reader. If one desires to be exposed to the innermost thoughts of an abused individual, then this is an appropriate book to read. We can all relate to some insecurity and we all can hide our truest feelings at times. But another person exposing them can make us all feel better. We all have to deal with difficult people, "bullies," whether they be other people or our own negative voices. Readers might find in this book a healing process due to her unfailing honesty. No one wants to feel like they are alone. Many people feel they are alone in their personal experiences, feelings, behaviors, and thoughts. But when we hear someone state the unspoken, the reaction on the part of the other is one of empowerment. This is why a book like this is necessary to read. We have to cease censoring ourselves and instead speak our inner voice. In addition, readers themselves who experienced bullying might feel better knowing they were not alone, even if in the midst of the bullying itself, they were alone externally.

In sum, *Blue and Gold* captures the feelings and experiences of an adolescent girl over a four-year period twenty-five years ago as she endured and suffered bullying at her high school. It reflects her emotional pressures at home, her struggles academically and socially, and her personal relationships with friends and bullying by enemies, with particular emphasis on the culture of a girls' school. It is a bleak and unforgiving landscape. One might have predicted that the bleakness would continue later in life—but the reader learns of the narrator's ultimate redemption through personal, social, and academic success. This is a reflective narrative of a wedge of life in which a sensitive girl experiences the "rite of passage" and struggles with the emotional and hormonal pressures of adolescence. For my own life, this book is helpful as I educate aspiring practitioners and the professors who teach them on how to empower clients and their families, including in schools. I recommend this book to you without reservation.

Manoj Pardasani, PhD, LCSW, ACSW
Senior Associate Dean
Fordham University Graduate School of Social Service

Prologue

My mother rode with me on three buses to demonstrate how I would be traveling to high school. She made it clear she would do this only once. The next time I was going to have to make the journey by myself. I'd never traveled alone before, and I couldn't believe I'd be doing it for the first time, for real, much sooner than I might have otherwise preferred. Especially with it being such a long journey, about an hour and a half in total.

I'd chosen the all-girls *Stella Maris*—Mary, Star of the Sea—school. Academics were not important to me; I simply wanted a school where I could make friends and take part in lots of extracurricular activities. I'd also been accepted into Alma Louis, another all-girls school, which had an excellent academic reputation. Unable to shake the sense that my parents were disappointed by my choice, I had to continually remind myself that they wanted me to make my own decisions when it came to this sort of thing.

I'd missed "Buddy Day," in which eighth graders who'd been accepted were given an all-day tour of the school and its classes by a senior. Due to not finding out about "Buddy Day" until it was too late, I wasn't permitted to experience or benefit from the tour. Following my persistence that I still wanted the tour, my father made a call to the assistant principal. I sat in the living room and listened to him arguing with her.

He finally said, "Do you realize that my daughter might choose your school over Alma Louis?"

Then, silence. He hung up the phone and told me it had been settled for me to visit.

Having already decided I wanted out of my current life, I also planned to recover from the disease of being "quiet," which was the label I'd always worn. I swore to myself that high school would be different. This time, I'd be well-liked by my peers, unlike my days in elementary school. I'd have friends. I'd have boyfriends. I'd dance and dance really well. Maybe, just maybe, I might even be happy.

And I was prepared to do whatever it took to achieve these goals.

Chapter 1

Freshman Year

The first few days of high school were a blur. It was all about me getting used to waking up at 5:45 a.m.—when it was still dark, for God's sake—and just dragging myself out of bed. I was fourteen and scared. I'd wake up congested every morning because it was so chilly, not helped by the fact that my bedroom was in the basement, making it extra dark. That was way too much of an adjustment for me, and to make matters worse, the rest of my family was still asleep, so I had to do it alone.

I hated seeing big bags under my eyes. I'd never had that before. I'd spend about an hour and a half getting ready, making a huge, huge fuss over every last detail of my appearance. I'd spend a ton of time blow-drying my hair before putting all sorts of chemicals in it like aerosol hairspray. I'd tease it up right on top of my head; this was the late eighties, after all, and teasing your hair as high as the sky was in style. Wearing a whole case of makeup was also in style. But completing this multitude of beauty treatments took forever.

When I got to the third bus stop, I'd usually see about a hundred girls in plaid uniforms smoking cigarettes. They'd be running around, talking and yelling. It looked like they were mostly Italian and Irish, and all were gorgeous beyond belief. A lot of them had the late eighties hair pulled up to high heaven and thick layers of makeup on, while others had their hair in simple ponytails with no makeup at all. When the bus finally came, we all crowded through the doorway, pushing each other to get inside.

The bus was crammed with girls, tightly squeezing in next to each other, leaving just enough room for the clouds of cigarette smoke to waft in between the bodies. The senior girls sat all the way in the back of the bus. The junior girls seemed to have their own section, too, as did the sophomores and us freshmen. It was a bitterly cold morning in September and still dark out. Being so exhausted, I couldn't help but feel like it was still nighttime—still *bedtime*! So, between listening to the loud shrieks and giggles of teen female voices and having to breathe in heavy second-hand smoke, I'd already decided it was way too much at such an early hour.

When we passed through Howard Beach, this scared, intimidated kind of numb feeling descended over me as the bus picked up the girls who lived there. Howard Beach was the town where that African American kid had been killed only a couple of years before, the incident led by John Lester. Howard Beach was mostly a wealthy area where Italian Mafia lived, as did the families of the people who took part in the incident. I couldn't believe I was going to be classmates with some of the offspring.

I looked at "these" girls as they got on the bus, and I didn't quite know what to make of them. High hair, of course, but they also had very long, colorful nails and lots of jewelry. Thankfully, they didn't give me the time of day.

As the bus traveled over a body of water, I realized I'd never traveled to school in this way before. This was also the first time I'd ever traveled by myself. It felt so stressful and weird, especially since the bridge was so close to the water.

We traveled through what looked like a poor neighborhood; mostly Irish working class at first, closely followed by the Hispanic and African American areas next. Then the bus crossed a larger body of water that led us to Rockaway Beach.

Finally arriving at school, all the freshmen were told they would each have a "Senior Sister" to accompany them on their so-called "Senior Sister Day." Senior sisters came around to all the freshmen homerooms first thing in the morning. I almost thought I wasn't going to have one, since virtually everyone else's had arrived and mine hadn't.

I sat patiently, waiting and waiting. The other freshmen in my class were already out of their seats and socializing with their senior sisters, whereas I remained in my front-row seat, by myself, and didn't say a word.

Just when I'd given up hope on having a guide for the day, a girl appeared in the doorway. "Hi, are you Mary Powell?" she asked.

"Yes," I replied.

She smiled and said, "I'm your senior sister."

I breathed a sigh of relief. Now I felt a pleasant sense of belonging, like I fit in. I wasn't going to stick out like a sore thumb after all.

At the end of my first day, I surveyed the first bus, seeing it was way too crowded, but managed to get a seat on the second. A girl with brown hair walked over and stopped at my seat. "Excuse me, can I sit here?"

I sensed by the way she asked that she wanted to be friends, so I flashed a nervous smile and shuffled over. As soon as she sat down, she proved to be extremely friendly and talkative. I, on the other hand, was shy and scared. Nevertheless, I was overjoyed that someone had made the first move to be friendly with me, because there's no way I would've done it if the tables were turned. Her name was Savannah.

As the first month wore on, I managed to pull off acquaintance-like conversations with a few girls in most of my classes, and I'd see

Savannah around to talk to here and there. Then, and I don't really know why, there was a couple of weeks where we didn't talk at all.

One sunny afternoon on the bus ride back home, I saw Savannah sitting alone. She looked me up and down as I approached. "Hi, Mary," she mumbled. The look on her face spoke volumes. Great, she knows I'm weird, and shy, and quiet, and a loser. That old story that follows me around everywhere. But I sat down next to her anyway, and we started talking. After that, Savannah and I wound up being best friends.

She and I became friendly with a girl named Cathy. She was tall with short frizzy blond hair and dark skin. Apparently, she was what they called a "metal head." She loved heavy metal music, although I didn't know what that was. When I asked her if the pop songs I liked were heavy metal, she looked like she might laugh in my face. Cathy was the sort of girl who wore black nail polish and wrote things like "Satan Rules" on her notebook. She was in a couple of classes with me, and all three of us were in Spanish class together.

I was placed in a "Regents" program, although I'd never heard of Regents either. It was a standardized test we'd all have to take for our major subjects at the end of the year. The teachers taught for the tests and the tests alone, not in a way where students might ever really learn the actual subject.

Art class. I'd always been talented in drawing; at least, that's what I'd always been told. In elementary school, I'd dazzled teachers and peers alike with cartoons and sketches of people, including people in my class. However, whenever my drawings were made the center of attention and given a positive response, I was usually overcome by embarrassment and shame. This was one way I unwittingly earned respect from other kids in my class.

In the eighth grade yearbook, I'd been awarded "Best Artist" along with "Most Quiet"—the latter of which came as no surprise.

Gym class was twice a week. I usually carried my shirt, shorts, and sneakers scrunched up in the bottom of a plastic grocery bag. I hated gym, I always had. In gym, there are no boundaries—no desks, no notebooks. It was a social event. Plus, I was terrible at sports and an awkward mover at the best of times. Because of that, no one ever wanted me on their team, so I always got picked last.

So many of the students seemed to like gym; it was a time to be athletic, to have fun, and to get away from classes. I always felt so painfully self-conscious and lonely, which invariably meant I ended up standing around by myself.

Also, this was the first time I'd ever had to change in front of other girls, right down to my bra and panties. In grade school, we'd just worn our gym clothes under our uniforms.

While everyone was seated in lines on the gym floor, a girl sat next to me and started talking to me—for all she knew, I was a normal girl! She was expecting a normal, easy conversation out of me at any second. And I knew I couldn't deliver. She was so pretty, and she looked so cool, so popular. I so wished I could've been friends with her. She wondered aloud what time it was. As a reflex, I looked at my wrist only to find I'd already taken it off. "Whoops!" I said. She laughed, and I laughed back. That was the last time we interacted.

Although we had a really sweet gym teacher, Ms. Rayfield, gym class still sucked. I only had a couple of friends in gym class and one of those was Cathy. She wasn't always around, though, so I'd often be left alone, shy as hell, while I watched the other students with curiosity and envy.

As I sat alone on the bleachers, a couple of really cool, super pretty girls sat near me talking to each other. Beauty-related stuff was the main topic of their conversation, and one of the girls explained how she shaved her legs every five days. I only wished

I had the discipline to shave my legs every five days. Deep down, I knew that's what I should've been doing, but I didn't. I felt like a loser, a failure. A dirty, unstylish girl.

I told myself these were the things that kept me unpopular, rather than the attractive, liked-by-everyone girl I wanted to be. Still, I kept not doing them, just like the years before. I couldn't understand why I didn't groom myself properly. Why couldn't I just be like these other girls and put my appearance first?

History. Another Regents class I couldn't stand and found too difficult. Social studies and history simply didn't interest me. It was too much to take in and remember. My concentration in that subject had never been very good. We were seated in a large, sunny classroom in alphabetical order, which meant I was sat toward the back, and one of the most popular girls in school, Emma, sat right in front of me.

The man who taught history was short, skinny, and had a slightly feminine look about him. His blond, long haircut sat rigid on top of his head and his glasses were always perched on the end of his nose. He had a low voice and almost zero charisma, but he always wore a shy smile.

It soon became apparent he had difficulty setting boundaries and enforcing discipline in our class, which was a shame because some students really needed it. He was dull and boring, and he got on my nerves. I had no respect for him, nor did the rest of the class.

Thankfully, both Savannah and Cathy were with me in English class. Sr. Rena was our teacher, an elderly, old-fashioned, angry specimen of a woman who made us pray before class. She regularly made some sort of speech about society that usually ended with, "This world's got to get its act together."

In one such English class, we watched a film version of *Romeo and Juliet*. After Romeo and Juliet had slept together for the first time, naked Romeo got up out of bed and stretched in front of the window. To see this naked guy with his bare ass stretching out right in front of me looked hilarious. I started to smirk. Oh no, please don't laugh, please don't, I told myself. That would be so embarrassing. Come on, I'm not five years old.

But I couldn't hold it in. I burst out laughing. In response, other people started to laugh, and before long, the whole room had erupted into fits of giggles. Cathy looked at me snickering.

"Oh, you people are so immature!" Sr. Rena hollered.

The laughing continued as Juliet rolled over to say hello to Romeo. We later remarked on how her entire chest was exposed.

Religion class. Our teacher, Ms. Peters, was short and chubby and she had a medium-length, blondish hairstyle that reminded me of the 1950s. She dressed it, too. Rumor had it that she was an ex-nun. Her attitude in general, including her attitude toward sex, was also stuck in the '50s. She was quite taken aback one day when it came to light that certain girls in our class had experience with kissing guys.

"So, are there seniors having sex?" she asked.

"Yeah!" virtually all the girls responded in a tone that suggested they couldn't believe Ms. Peters didn't know.

"Well, not freshmen, surely," she said, gasping.

The class responded emphatically, "Yeah! I know girls who are..."

"Oh my goodness, oh my goodness!" At that point, I thought she was going to faint.

While not shocked to the verge of passing out, I had to admit that I, too, was astonished by the girls' response. It was really hard to believe girls in high school were actually *having sex*. And freshmen too? I had a sense it was not many, but still. How could anyone be in such a serious relationship already? These girls must have proper boyfriends to be doing that with them. Yuck. I couldn't imagine myself in that sort of commitment right now. We're so young! I guess these girls are more mature? "Older" psychologically? The image of a Stella girl being sexually involved and seriously committed; it was so strange, sickening, and just unfamiliar. It didn't feel good.

Ms. Peters seemed so curious about which students in her class had been physically involved with a guy that a couple of the girls got excited. One of them started an impromptu activity and said to the class, "Let's find out how many of us have ever kissed a boy. But I mean *really* kissed a boy, *deep* kissing, using your tongue."

A couple of the other students joined in and instructed the class to write down on a piece of paper "yes" or "no" to indicate whether or not they had "ever kissed a boy—deep kissed." Everyone was all into it and laughing.

Ms. Peters simply stepped aside and watched.

I was embarrassed to the point where I'd wished for the ground to open up and swallow me whole. Really, I'd never put much thought into the fact that I'd never kissed someone, but now I got the sense that not having kissed a boy by fourteen was apparently pathetic. Here I was, the odd one out—again.

As a few of the students handed out pieces of paper, I pondered a question of my own. Should I lie and write yes? I felt like the whole class was watching me. I'd always had this problem, feeling like the whole world was watching my actions, judging me like an audience about to cast a vote against their least favorite contestant on a TV show.

Of course, nobody would know who it was if I wrote "no." Nor would they know if I lied and wrote "yes." I felt like such a loser. I was the reason I'd never kissed a boy. It was because of me—I was ugly, shy, and weird.

I snapped myself back to reality and realized that no one in the class was watching me. They weren't watching anyone for that matter because they were too busy with their own pieces of paper. I had to remind myself it was anonymous, and no one would know. Plus, there had to be other girls who hadn't made out with a guy. We were only fourteen, I told myself, and anyway, lying was wrong. It went against my beliefs and my heart.

Since I couldn't get myself to lie, I scribbled "no" on my paper and folded it up. With the pieces of paper handed in, my only fear was that they would recognize my handwriting. Perhaps worse still, they'd make the judgment that ugly Mary Powell obviously had to be one of the girls who hadn't kissed a guy.

After the couple of girls in charge had counted up the answers, they announced that only two girls had written "no." The rest were "yes." Automatically, I felt like I didn't fit in; I'd never fit in, I was developmentally failing, inadequate, stupid. What a loser I was. From then on, I figured I needed to really get a move on with finding a boyfriend or at least making out with a guy.

Sr. Helena was my math class teacher. She was a short elderly nun with a limp. Some people said she had alcohol on her breath at times, but that was just a rumor; she could've just come out of mass—who knows? I wound up being her scapegoat, and everyone knew it. I figured it was for several reasons. One, I was a social nobody and she picked it up. Two, because she got away with picking on me, I let her do it. And three, because I performed so terribly in her class.

The girls in the class would laugh at Sr. Helena's teaching style. We'd imitate her voice and her strange actions. We'd mimic how, whenever someone gave the wrong answer, Sr. Helena would pretend to play a violin, and she talked weird most of the time.

It was all pretty hysterical until she started to pick on me instead. She'd come right up to my desk and ask me a question.

When I didn't know the answer, she'd say negative things and ask even more questions just to put me on the spot and embarrass me. At one point, when I answered a question wrong in a shy, terrified manner, she announced that my seat would be moved to the front of the classroom by her desk.

The entire class yelled out, "Oooohhh!"

I'd never been spoken to or humiliated by a teacher like that before. I'd always done my best with my work and behaved well in class. I felt traumatized. Yet, I said nothing.

Science class, taught by Ms. Robertson, took place in a lab. We sat two by two at long tables, in alphabetical order by last name. I sat next to an Irish girl named Jordan. She, like me, seemed reserved and quiet. We barely said hello at any of our classes.

I constantly felt like I didn't know what the hell I was doing in science. The material felt too difficult, too much, too overwhelming. Our teacher would holler the material at us from across the room, expecting us to absorb everything without question. I didn't get what these Regents were all about. What were they? What would be on them? Despite my endless confusion, my fellow classmates seemed to catch on and follow the lesson with ease.

One time, Ms. Robertson had me stand at the front of the enormous lab in front of my entire science class. She instructed me to try to work out a problem with her while everyone watched. When I demonstrated that I didn't know what I was doing, snickers started to ripple out across the room behind me. She looked at the class and said, "Don't laugh, because every dog has his day."

What does *that* mean? Whether she was trying to help or not, it didn't feel good. I felt like crap, as usual. Humiliated, as usual.

Ms. Robertson seemed to have a favoritism thing for Savannah. She also seemed to have a thing for Emma, who sat up front only because her surname happened to appear earlier in the alphabet.

Emma was an Irish freshman girl with beautiful brown hair. She was most definitely one of the popular ones. Given that she was in several of my classes, I saw a lot of her. I thought she was begrudgingly pretty—or at least her hair was. Her long brown hair was cut and styled in a way that was considered cool. For reasons unbeknown to me, she didn't seem to need to put in any hairspray or anything; whichever way she fashioned her hair, it looked great. She could put it in a ponytail, leave it out, have it in a total mess on top of her head, it didn't matter, it still looked amazing.

Emma also seemed, to me anyway, like she was a first-class bitch. She was incredibly loud, mean, and didn't appear to associate with anyone other than her own crowd. In science class, though, possibly because her friends weren't there or maybe due to the strict seating Ms. Robertson had us in, Emma kept quiet and slumped over. She always looked exhausted and hungover when she sat in class.

Ms. Robertson would pick on her, too, but her teasing seemed to be delivered with affection where Emma was concerned. I also think Emma was intimidated by her, as most students were, so she wouldn't say much back. After Ms. Robertson called her "dizzy," it became her nickname for the rest of the year.

In most other classes, Emma was entirely different. She was her usual loud self. She socialized with her friends, played pranks, and joked around. I longed to be social too, mainly so Emma would like me. Instead, I'd sit in my seat, silent, embarrassed and conscious of how my body looked to those around me.

One thing I had decided to do to improve my appearance was I'd started to wear tights and socks underneath my uniform skirt. The other girls no doubt laughed about it behind my back, but I thought it looked cool.

Ms. Robertson was irritated by how I was performing on

my Regents practice tests. She wasn't thrilled with my lack of participation in class, or, it seemed, just me in general. She would make loud comments to express her disgust with me. For example, my locker was totally disorganized. There were piles of books, gym clothes, old lunch, God knows what, all stacked on top of each other.

Savannah and I were by my open locker one time when Ms. Robertson stopped by and started talking to Savannah. I knelt down to find something in my locker-mountain, and as I pulled out a book, everything else slid down and spewed out across the floor.

With a look of repulsion, Ms. Robertson said, "When are you going to get yourself together?" I felt embarrassed and ashamed, like a slob and a mess and a total failure. I wasn't doing things right, I thought. I was doing everything wrong.

Soon after the locker incident, the first parent-teacher night took place. This gave the parents an opportunity to talk to the teachers alone, without the students in the room. As I passed by the science classroom, I saw Ms. Robertson talking to my parents. They were silent, and Ms. Robertson had an "I'm really concerned... She is going to fail...She is a problem...I've had it" look on her face as she talked. A bad feeling stirred in the pit of my stomach. That woman just did not like me, I thought. It reminded me that I was a screw-up. Abnormal. Different. Wrong.

As my parents drove me home, I noticed they were on the quiet side. My mother said she was annoyed at some of my teachers, particularly Ms. Robertson, who had said she would tutor me as long as my parents paid for it. They'd refused. My mother said it was terrible she would charge students like that.

My parents had also talked to Sr. Helena, who said that I was failing math and that I should drop out of the Regents program because it was probably too difficult for me. When I heard that, well, I refused to even think about quitting.

Despite my shaky belief in my intelligence, I knew in my heart that I was smart enough to get through it. I'd had insecure thoughts that everyone else was doing exceedingly well compared to me but, in reality, just about everyone in the Regents program was having some degree of difficulty. And just about everyone in the whole school was in the Regents program, so there was no reason I couldn't be, too. Only students with severe learning difficulties were in the non-Regents program. So, no, I was not about to listen to any crap about dropping out.

"She has a mental block in math," Sr. Helena had said to my mother. That hurt. Mainly because I knew it wasn't true. I had performed well in math when I was younger. It was her, not me! It was her awful way of teaching.

My mother went on to explain how she'd gotten into an argument with Sr. Helena, who'd responded, "Don't tell me how to teach or do my job." Knowing my mother had "told her how to teach" made me feel great.

My mother knew what she was talking about when it came to these things, since she was a certified teacher herself. She was confident and assertive, and although I didn't always like to admit it, she was usually also right. I knew that was probably why Sr. Helena responded the way she had. My mother had told her the correct way to teach. Not that it would make any difference; she wouldn't change.

I felt stuck. I had to go back to that class, day in, day out, for the rest of the year. I had to suffer. The image of the class, Sr. Helena and the way she taught, the Regents, all my other subjects, freshman year in general, high school, adolescence, everything—it was all so traumatic. I didn't know how to feel or what to think.

*　　*　　*

For the remainder of the year, I stayed shy, wrapped up in my own bubble of insecurity, and the other freshman girls proved to be way out of my league. The closest contact I had with any of them was when I took the smoky bus to and from Rockaway and heard them yelling and laughing. I definitely did not exist to them. If Savannah or Cathy wasn't with me on the bus, it was guaranteed to be an incredibly lonely ride.

My desire to be popular and make friends with these girls was waning. I could sense they would never give me the time of day. They seemed so different from me, like they were from another world, a world that existed only to them. They shared some sort of secret language all of their own. I heard weekend plans and I heard them say things, good and bad, about other girls from class. The good things they said were exceptionally good, but the bad things they said were painfully, shockingly bad. Some girls they talked about were "wonderful," while others were "sluts," or "skanks," or "nerds." Some were going to get "whacked" or "had better watch it."

After school one day, I met Savannah's family for the first time. They had a last name that I teased her about affectionately and she would feign offense each time. Savannah had a sister, Jetta, who was two years her junior and hung out with us whenever I went over. Savannah's mother was very talkative, albeit a little on the loud side, but then again, the whole family was somewhat aggressive when it came to asserting their points of view; borderline angry.

Throughout elementary school, I suffered with the ups and downs of depression, and my constant anxiety left me with little energy to do my homework or study. The main reason I scored acceptable to high grades in elementary school was because my mother and father had forced me to do my work. There were times they practically did the work for me.

My parents stopped their assistance when I started high school. Cold turkey, basically. I was on my own. They had started to wean me off their help when I was in junior high, and my grades had dropped from As and B+s to Bs and Cs. They barely helped me at all in high school unless I asked. I felt like there was a hole underneath me. No grounding. All alone, with no one to fend for me. No one to help me. Nowhere to turn. Confusion. What the fuck?

It was like a void around me, a space. A constant cloudy day. In school, I only really had one close friend. Savannah. No one else—teacher or student—seemed to want to get close to me. I felt like a second grader in a college classroom. What was this strange world? The only thing I knew was that I was alone. Unworthy of having a lot of friends. As usual.

Chapter 2

I was often late for school because I had such a hard time getting out of bed in the morning. And because I'd take a ridiculous amount of time to get ready.

Try as I might, I had no idea what the hell I was doing as I spiked my hair up in a late-eighties Guidette style. All the other girls' hair came out perfect when they did it, or at least the way it was supposed to come out. When I finished mine, I'd think it looked great, but really, it was hideous. Other girls made fun of it. I'd put half of my hair back and keep some of it down, but the front bangs would be standing straight up like daggers. Worse still, the hairspray created a whole heap of flakes that looked like dandruff.

Once, I was in the girls' bathroom at the same time as an older girl. As I was standing in front of the mirror washing my hands, she confirmed my insecurity about my attempted hairstyle. "How come your hair doesn't do this?" she said, gesturing with her hand down her forehead. Meaning, why were my bangs standing straight up? She laughed and walked away before I had the chance to think of an answer. I didn't even try to stand up for myself. But, then again, I never did.

When Christmas came, my few friends and I got each other presents. I didn't have much money, so I didn't get anyone fancy presents, but I was able to get them all a little something. It felt exciting to have friends in the first place to get presents for.

Savannah and I were almost the last students in the building before leaving for the holidays. She was in her homeroom talking to Ms. Robertson. I still felt really weird about Ms. Robertson, so I waited outside in the hall. It was strange how Ms. Robertson loved my best friend but not me.

As Savannah came out of the classroom, in a quiet and somewhat condescending voice, she said, "Ms. Robertson has something for you."

Ms. Robertson stood at her desk, eyeing me suspiciously as I walked in. She was half-smiling. "I have a present for you," she said before handing me a Christmas tree ornament and kissing me on the cheek. I was shocked to say the least. "Have a great Christmas, dizzy," she added as I left the room.

I loved it when she called me that. Being known as dizzy certainly makes you stand out, doesn't it? That, I loved.

I was being seen as a dumb girl—dumb girls were popular and not geeks. That, I loved. And she only called a few select people "dizzy," meaning I was one of her favorites. That, I also loved.

*   *   *

Sooner or later, I learned that I had to talk; I'd have to start socializing if I wanted to fit in with them. I couldn't just sit there trying to be "cool" forever. I'd already failed at that. I procrastinated. I waited and waited but didn't open my mouth. Time passed. I couldn't talk to them. I didn't know how. I felt frozen. And, one day, a student in my history class said, "You're too quiet, Mary. You gotta perk up."

Emma, without even looking at me, readily agreed and said, "Yeah. You gotta perk up!"

Okay, so now it's official, I thought. I've fucked it up here, too.

I'd done it again. Now they all knew I was a quiet little dork and it was only a matter of time before it started to get around. Wherever I went, it never changed. They were right, I was a failure. I wasn't perky. I wasn't happy and "with it."

But I couldn't. I just couldn't. I was tired. Plus, these girls were truly scary. To me, they were offensive and intimidating. There was something strange and unfamiliar about them. I had been around mean, popular girls all my life, but these ones seemed to be on a whole new level of extreme with their cruelty. It was like something was terribly, horribly wrong.

These girls seemed to have hearts that were made of solid stone. But I still thought it was me with the problem, that it was me who had to shape up and get with the program, that it was me who had deficits in her social skills. I didn't know how to stand up for myself, nor did I have the confidence to begin a conversation. But I could see that even if I learned how to, in this particular environment, it would not matter. Once I was deemed "not part of their crowd" and already labeled as "strange," it was pretty much too late.

As freshman year wore on, I spent more and more time with Savannah and we became closer than ever. However, as we became closer, she started to annoy me. Her sister too. But what could I do? She was one of my only friends in school, so I simply tried to ignore my feelings.

It was right around this time when I found out that a cousin of one of my old friends from junior high, Christy, who lived around my block, was in my year. I was at Savannah's locker once, and a chubby girl with light skin and dark red hair walked by. "Do you know Christy?" she asked.

"Yeah," I replied.

She smiled at me and said, "I'm her cousin Judy." She was really friendly. We exchanged a few more words and that was it. But, soon after this, I noticed she started giving me the cold shoulder and I didn't know why.

There were a couple of times after that when I passed Christy and her cousin Judy in the neighborhood. I'd pluck up the courage to say hi, but in return, they would just stare at me.

I was confused. Christy used to be my friend. We'd drifted apart simply because we went to different high schools, not because any animosity had developed. I'd thought we always liked hanging out and enjoyed each other's company. I knew that if Christy took a disliking to someone, she could be extra mean to them, so I certainly wouldn't have ever wanted to get on her bad side. Because I was starting to feel afraid of Christy and Judy, I'd always think twice before going out on the streets just in case I ran into them.

Then there was Jake, another kid in the neighborhood who had been one of my brother's friends for a short time. He was a couple of years younger than me, but he'd been to my house a few times to hang out.

Honestly, I thought he was really annoying. He and my brother James got on really well, but Jake liked to pick on my younger brother Ted—as did the rest of us at times.

Once, while I was at home, I heard that he'd held Ted's head under the water at a pool. As I pictured Jake doing this to my little brother over and over in my head, I became so angry that I lost control. I grabbed a baseball bat in the living room.

My little sister Andrea saw me and ran up to me. "What are you doing? What are you doing?"

"I'm going after that fucking asshole!" I said.

I'd never gotten aggressive like that before. I left the house and ran up my block before looking all over for Jake, my sister following me in a panic. After ten minutes of searching, I found Jake hanging out with his friends.

As soon as I laid eyes on him, I started screaming at him about the pool incident. When he saw the baseball bat, he jumped on his bike and started to pedal away down the street.

"Get off the fucking bike!" I yelled.

"No, I won't!" he shouted back over his shoulder.

"Of course, because you're a fucking chicken. You stay the fuck away from my brother! Alright? Or I swear to God, I'll kick your ass!"

"Oh shut up, bitch."

As I stared at this kid on his bike, I knew there was nothing he could do to me. He was smaller, I had a bat, and I was being scary. I was glad. This was the first time I'd ever taken the role of aggressor, rather than victim, and I was proud of it. For once, I was the bully, I sounded cool, and I loved every second of it. He'd been beaten. He was scared of me. Watching with delight as he scurried away on his little bike, I figured he'd never try that crap again.

But, despite my sudden outburst of confidence, things started to get difficult for me around my neighborhood. I guess word had spread about what happened with Jake, and now some other guys were making harsh comments about me, to me, and that really hurt. But, even worse, whenever I passed by Christy and Judy, they would stop talking, stare at me with smirks, and I'd hear them laughing and snickering about me. What's going on? What happened? What did I do to make Christy hate me? Did her cousin say something about me?

It hurt like hell, especially because it was Christy. We'd been friends since junior high school and I liked her so much. I liked her family, too. Her sister and my sister had been best friends.

I found out later there was another Stella girl who lived on my block, but she took a different route to school so I'd never seen much of her before. One time, we passed each other as I was walking home. "Do you go to Stella Maris?" she asked, walking across the street toward me.

"Yeah," I replied nervously.

She laughed. "Well, obviously you do, since you're wearing the same uniform as me. What's your name?"

"Um, it's Mary."

"I'm Jodi," she replied, smiling.

"Wow, I can't believe you live all the way out here, and right across the street from me, too," I said.

"Well, it's nice to meet you."

"You too," I said as she waved and walked away to her house.

Much to my surprise, the impromptu interaction with Jodi wasn't hard. She definitely didn't seem like one of "those" girls at Stella. I wondered if we'd ever be friends. After all, she did live right there across the street.

I also got to know another sophomore named Lana. She often seemed to be somewhat hyper and preoccupied, but she started to show an interest in hanging out with me. I was thoroughly flattered by her company because she was really pretty and cool, and she was a sophomore. There was usually a group of friends with her, too, which gave me more connections and an opportunity to walk around with a crowd. It made me look and feel more popular than ever.

Latching on with Lana and her friends, I thought my social life would pick up in some ways. While my skills in conversing weren't great, these girls just giving me a chance to hang around them without being rejected or made fun of was gradually building up my confidence. I figured it was perfect. This was how to do it. A gradual growth. First, just being accepted. Second, just hanging around with them. Then, and only then, I'd work on what to actually say.

Even though I had my foot in the door with a new group of girls, I'd always sort of "go home" to Savannah. She was already my best friend, so I knew I didn't have to worry about losing her. That helped. I'd never had that kind of security in school before.

The only downfall with Savannah was that, at times, she'd criticize me. Especially when she was around her sister, who could be harsh and judgmental. Their jokes were sometimes funny, but other times, they could be a little insulting and hurtful.

While I was making more friends, I was also starting to make some enemies at Stella. I suppose they were the girls who'd figured out I was shy, weird, disheveled, and a pushover. Maria. She was the worst. A hideously ugly girl in my homeroom, she was also in my religion and gym classes. For whatever reason, she just hated me. She made fun of me and insulted me and apparently just detested me.

One day, I came to my locker and I found a long note. *You are a pain in a lot of people's asses, did you know that?...You are so ugly... You wear too much makeup...You look like a clown...You would be perfect for a clown in the circus...* It went on and on with a list of angry, spiteful comments. I felt devastated. I figured it had to be Maria.

It hurt like hell, but a small part of me—albeit a minuscule, microscopically small part—was not hurt in the slightest. After all, only one person had written that note. If only one person hated me, really hated me, obviously there had to be something wrong with them—not me.

There was a girl named Caitlin in a few of my classes: religion, art, and math. She had long dark hair and was fairly quiet most of the time. She didn't seem shy in the same way I was. Rather, she seemed like someone who just wanted to get her work done and stay out of trouble. I also had a feeling she wanted to protect herself from the abuse a student might receive if they drew attention to themselves.

There was a girl in my math class who also was very quiet, but also kind of geeky looking. Her short blond hair was kind of messy and she wore glasses. Virtually everyone struggled in this math class, but this particular girl was extremely bright.

I felt a twinge of envy that this nerdy girl got it, but I knew that was my issue, not hers. Several other girls, however, were not so subtle. A few of them would vehemently scoff at her out loud for having the right answer.

One of the popular girls who had a reputation for having incredibly gorgeous hair—personally I didn't think it was so great, but everyone else did—looked straight over in this nerdy girl's direction. She flicked her long hair over her shoulder and gave nerdy girl a disapproving look. "Oh my god!" she growled under her breath. It was like nerdy girl had done something terribly wrong just by getting the answer right.

Chapter 3

I was taking a lot of sick days in freshman year, mostly because I had a lot of trouble getting myself out of bed at 5:30 a.m. I'd faked various illnesses many times and had my mother call the school to say I was sick. I tried to tell myself I'd earned a break, but I didn't believe it deep down.

I knew my rationale was dysfunctional and could land me in trouble. This had never happened to me in elementary school—lateness, sick days, falling behind academically. I'd spend a lot of time in bed, getting as much sleep as I needed. I'd sleep for at least the whole morning, sometimes it ended up being well into the afternoon.

Also, I'd learned I could use the nurse's office to my advantage. Previously, I'd thought a nurse's office was for injuries or emergencies. But, if I got to a class and felt exhausted or just felt like I couldn't tolerate the other girls, I'd walk up to the teacher's desk, put on a "sick" face, and ask for a note to the nurse's office. My theatrics worked more often than not.

After the nurse had taken me in and given me the once over, I'd spend the entire class period trying to get some sleep on one of the couches in her office. Although I enjoyed the rest, I always felt guilty. I thought about the work I was missing and that I could be failing as a result, but I was exhausted, too. My fatigue was starting to scare me. I'd lie there thinking about how miserable high school and life in general was making me.

When I first started faking being sick, my friends, thinking I really was sick, were sympathetic and supportive. I once bumped into Cathy in the hall after I'd missed Spanish and had gone to the nurse's office, and she asked me what was wrong. When I told her I wasn't feeling well, she said with concern and affection, "Oh, my poor sick child!"

But, as time went on and I continued this behavior, that concern and care from my friends started to fade. It was humiliating because I knew they knew I was faking the whole thing. I hated the idea that my friends could be thinking negatively about me or rejecting me in any way.

Both Savannah and I went to the nurse's office together one day. She wasn't feeling well. Me, I was just tired and wanted to hang with her. And I couldn't face a class. Savannah told the nurse her stomach was hurting and that she didn't know what was going on. The nurse asked her if she had her period.

Oh my god! Period! That's so weird, was my first thought. Someone, my friend, having her period. I hadn't gotten mine yet. Savannah said that no, she didn't have her period. Oh, okay, she didn't get hers yet either. Good. I didn't realize, though, that what Savannah meant was that no, she didn't have her period at that moment in time.

I was fourteen and didn't have my period yet. And I had no breasts. My friend from elementary school, Rebecca, had called me up one night, saying, "Guess what?"

"What?" I asked, excited to hear whatever news it was she had.

"I got my period," she announced, sounding extremely proud.

I had been shocked and scared for her, imagining her getting her first period and bleeding. I felt like a freak. Fourteen and no period. Not that I really wanted it. I just thought I should have it.

It wasn't too long after that when I was on the toilet, thankfully at home, and I looked down at the toilet paper in my hand. I saw a faded, tiny mark of red. It was so light I could barely see it, so I really didn't think it was my period. Nevertheless, I called my mother and showed it to her. She looked at me, smiled, and confirmed that I'd started. I was confused, but it didn't feel as scary as I thought it would be. She gave me a maxi pad.

I wore one pad, thinking that was enough. On the second day, I started bleeding a lot—literally all over the freaking place. I had to go to the bathroom constantly to clean up. I could even feel the blood come out. I'd go to the bathroom and blood would be on my butt. My butt was bleeding!

"Mom! Is my butt supposed to be bleeding?" She assured me it was perfectly normal and that yes that could happen.

Then, in math class, I felt a ton of blood gush down into my pad and it didn't seem to stop. Oh dear God.

When the bell rang at the end of class, I got up and there was blood on the chair. I was beyond humiliated; I was mortified and more than ready to die right that second. I shoved the chair under the desk and got the hell out of there. There was no way I was going to let anyone see what I'd left behind on my seat. The next student who sat at that desk was just going to have to deal with it.

I went to the bathroom and checked my clothes. Fortunately, my uniform had a dark gray, plaid skirt, and the round spot the blood had left was only small, about the size of two quarters. I turned my skirt so the brownish mark was facing the side in the hopes it might look like some other kind of stain, rather than a period leak.

As I started walking to the table for my lunch, my stupid friends, especially Savannah, noticed the stain from about five feet away. They started cracking up. I was shocked. How did they see it? I'd thought it wasn't that noticeable. When they asked me what the stain was, I tried to make something up about a leaky marker pen, but it didn't work. My stain was the highlight of their day and became their favorite joke for the rest of the week. To say I was embarrassed would've been an understatement.

I told my mother what happened as soon as I arrived home. In a slightly critical tone, she told me I needed to wear two pads during my heaviest days, one covering the front side and one covering the back. From then on, I never failed to wear the requisite two pads, even on my lighter days, just to be sure.

*　　*　　*

Driving home one day, my father expressed how he and my mother were becoming increasingly angry and disappointed with me about my grades. He reminded me, over and over, that performing well grade-wise had never been my priority.

Pointing at me over his shoulder, he yelled, "No, you said, and I quote, 'The reason I am going to high school is to make friends and be popular'!" He was just awful.

The argument continued when we arrived home. My mother yelled at me in disgust, "All your friends are going to be doctors, and you'll be working at McDonald's!"

I stayed silent. She scared me. I thought she might have a point, but a part of me disagreed with her. That wasn't really going to happen. I knew my life had purpose and meaning, but I couldn't help fearing that maybe she was right. It wasn't that I wasn't smart, it was that I simply couldn't grasp the whole Regents idea. Admittedly, I knew I wasn't trying hard enough or studying the right way, but for me, the material was just too hard and too boring.

My parents were very involved in the Catholic church. My mother, before meeting my father, had been a nun for ten years. My father, before meeting my mother, had been in the Jesuit seminary to become a priest. But he didn't go ahead with the ordination, and my mother eventually left the sisterhood. They later met in graduate school for psychology.

Thanks to both of their backgrounds, I was brought up in a pretty religious environment. I felt lucky to have parents who instilled religion in me and had no doubts or questions about my faith.

During my childhood, up until I was twelve, my family and I had lived in a Hasidic and Orthodox Jewish neighborhood. The residents didn't have anything to do with us because we weren't Jewish. They acted as though we didn't exist. After finally winning the battle to make a few friends in the area, my father explained to my siblings and I that the Jewish parents were not allowing their children to play with us anymore. Apparently, this was because they were in fear of inter-faith marriage. It was devastating for me. I really liked them. That left us with no friends in the neighborhood at all.

As a child, I finished up believing that Jewish people were the "enemy" of Christianity. My faith was the most important thing in the world to me. It was one of the few things that made me happy. I believed they were wrong while we were right. That we were better than them. The schools I went to reinforced this childhood belief with occasional, slightly negative comments about the Jewish religion. For the most part, other religions were ignored altogether. There was no doubting or questioning of Catholicism allowed. You just didn't do it.

*   *   *

Gym class continued to be a torturous time for me. Girls who had talked to me at the beginning of the year, now laughed at me and made fun of me. One day, me and a bunch of girls sat in the bleachers waiting for class to start. Among them was a girl named Roberta.

Roberta tapped me on the shoulder and asked, "Do you give blow jobs?"

I had no idea what that was. What was she talking about? I knew she was making fun of me, so I wanted to think of a quick comeback. But I was scared and shy. All I could muster was, "Do you?"

Several of them laughed at me. She asked again, "Do you give blow jobs?"

I didn't know what to say. "Do you?" I repeated. They laughed even more.

Another said, "She probably doesn't even know what it is anyway." They all fell about in fits of giggles. I felt humiliated. Were they going to ask me what it was now? She was right; I had no clue. I felt scared. Fortunately, they didn't ask.

Maria, the student in my religion and gym class who seriously hated me, began picking on me at every possible opportunity. But, whenever she made fun of the way I looked, I'd smile to myself and think about how she really wasn't one to talk. She had to be the most unattractive girl in school. She looked like a goddamn boy. Her hair was crew-cut, she wore glasses, and she was bony. The sight of her disgusted me, so I guessed we were pretty much on the same wavelength about each other. The only difference was that I never picked on her. I wouldn't dare.

Most of the other females in school also continued to harass me. I once ran down the hallway steps and jumped over the last couple. It had become a habit of mine. Sr. Helena was sitting at a table at the bottom of the stairs, which was set up for the faculty member in charge of lunch period. She scolded me for the way I'd hurried down the stairs. Her punishment was for me to go back upstairs and come down again, this time in a quieter, more ladylike fashion. Fueled by anger, I stomped back upstairs. I then purposely tiptoed back down to go to the cafeteria. As I passed Sr. Helena, she commented on how I'd walked up the stairs like an elephant and then back down like a ballerina.

One day, I was absent from school without my parents knowing. I'd forged my mother's signature on the absentee note. I thought my handwriting was very similar to hers, but it got figured out in the end.

My mother reprimanded me, but I didn't get punished by either her or the school. However, I did get a long talk from a nun who assisted the principal. I wasn't really listening to her, but I did at least pretend to. When she finally stopped preaching, out of absolutely nowhere, she studied me and said, "You're very pretty."

I felt uncomfortable. It didn't feel like a compliment. It felt condescending. This was a time for me where, if an adult told me I was pretty, it somehow meant I looked like my mother. It meant I was pretty in a different way from other girls. It made me feel guilt and shame, like I had some powerful quality that was considered inappropriate. I didn't care if an adult thought I was pretty; their opinion didn't count. Only my peers' opinions mattered to me. I didn't want to be near that woman again. Not too long after that incident, she died.

*   *   *

As my grades continued to slide, I became more and more depressed. I was focusing so much on getting myself out of trouble in math that I started neglecting my other studies, which is what made my overall grades lower. It was traumatizing and shocking at the same time. Academically, I'd always done well before high school. How could I be failing? I told myself it was because I was a failure in general. It felt like my life was falling apart.

Sr. Deborah, our guidance counselor, was a skinny, waddling nun with large breasts that virtually hung down to the floor. She always wore ugly skirt suits and her dark hair was always cut short. She never wore a habit.

When she expressed her concern about my grades, I told her, feeling stupid to say so, about my troubles in math and that's why I thought my other grades were suffering. I felt ridiculous. It made no sense to spend so much time on one subject while your other grades suffered.

During the session, I broke down in tears and told her the other reasons why I was unhappy. I explained to her all about how the other students didn't like me and picked on me constantly. Hearing my stories, she seemed to show me a little more compassion. I told her I was seriously considering leaving and transferring to public school.

As I sat in tears with Sr. Deborah, she rambled on, trying to counsel me. While discussing my emotional state, the word "depression" was used. She said in a matter-of-fact tone, "It comes and goes with the weather." I looked outside and, ironically, it was pouring. That couldn't be it, I thought. I'd felt like this on sunny days, too.

She ended with, "And I'd be sorry to see you go."

The sincerity in her voice actually made me feel special. Okay, maybe I should stay, I thought. It felt nice to hear such words.

Thinking of the couple of friends I had made me realize I couldn't leave. I knew Savannah would miss me. She might even feel hurt or abandoned.

I stayed, just like I knew I would.

Chapter 4

Much to the dismay of my parents and teachers, I started dressing more and more provocatively. My clothes became increasingly non-existent. As did most of my student cohorts, I rolled up my uniform skirt as far as I could and rolled down my knee socks to expose more leg. Whenever we were told to fix them back, we'd only rolled everything back up and down the way we had them as soon as the teacher turned away.

Once, I came to school on a "no uniform" day in a denim skirt. As I bent down by my locker, another student yelled nastily, "Hey, girl, where's the rest of your skirt?" I felt ashamed.

However, after years of being viewed like a dork and feeling sick of it, I happily welcomed any other kind of label. The idea of being viewed as a "slut" suddenly became appealing.

I found out that Stella had a major event, an annual competition in April, called "Blue and Gold." Blue and gold were the school colors. The blue team was composed of freshmen and seniors. The gold team was composed of sophomores and juniors. Anyone in the school could join in. The teams would compete in dance, aerobics, gymnastics, art, and other activities. We could join as many teams as we wanted. Every year, Blue and Gold had a different theme. This year, the blue team's theme was "Madonna," so, naturally, the team song had to be Madonna.

My senior sister Lydia and her best friend were also in Blue and

Gold, but they were on the art team. The art teams were challenged to each make a banner representing Blue and Gold, decorated according to their theme. Blue's banner would have a Madonna theme. The gold team's theme was the movie *Flashdance*, so their banner would have a *Flashdance* theme.

Being a freshman, I'd be on the blue team, and I decided to join the dance team. I don't know what possessed me to join the dance team, given I couldn't dance to save my life, but to me, dancing was the key to being cool. And I just liked music and dancing. Plus, Blue and Gold sounded awesome. It sounded better than any other competition I'd ever been in during elementary school, where they almost always did sports and left me feeling bad about myself for not fitting in.

The captains of the teams were seniors, with a freshman assistant captain. Danielle, an Irish girl with short blond hair, one of the most popular girls, was the freshman assistant for my dance team. She was by far the best dancer, too. She was also in my gym class. I would sit and watch Danielle with a huge smile on her face, clearly loving being the center of attention like she was a famous actress. I didn't see what was so special, but apparently a pack of girls in gym class did.

Everyone in the blue team picked up the dance pretty easily. I was the only one struggling and it was highly embarrassing. Why couldn't I dance? God, I couldn't move my body with any sort of coordination. How did people just get on and dance with all the right steps and arm movements like it was nothing?

All the captains of Blue and Gold were completely engrossed in the competition. It seemed to absorb every moment of the students' lives, and they wanted nothing but to win. We practiced a couple of times a week after school from January to April. Sometimes, we would end up practicing in the school hallway; there was only one gym and it was often occupied.

I was tired and drained during practice one day, but one of the girls on our team was obviously feeling appreciative of one of the dance captains, Patty, although I didn't know why. She was jumping up and down while shouting, "Yay, everybody clap for Patty! Everybody!" All the girls put their hands up to clap. I just stood there with an "oh give me a break" look plastered across my face. I was too exhausted to put up my hands to clap for no apparent reason. As soon as this other girl noticed my lack of participation, she clenched her teeth and yelled at me, "Do it. Do it now, bitch." A couple of the other girls laughed as I reluctantly did as she said.

Patty taught us a dance step that she wanted us to master. So much so that she had each one of us do it solo while the rest of the team stood back to observe. I watched each girl complete the dance, and then it came to one particular freshman girl who never bothered to even look at me, let alone talk to me. She did a super cute version of the move, but I hated the look on her annoying face while she did it. She acted like she were some sort of fucking princess. It was a sickening display.

When it came to my turn to do it in front of everyone, I couldn't for the life of me get it right. And I was the only one who messed it up. We continued the practice with the music, and I saw one of the assistant captains whispering something to the teacher in charge while looking at me. They were both shaking their heads. So, I was officially a problem to the dance team. You're supposed to join a dance team because you can dance. I joined because I *wanted* to. Because I thought it was cool, because I was trying to prove something to myself. I was trying to be someone I wasn't.

Thrown off by these two humiliating incidents, I took matters into my own hands—I practiced my ass off at home. Hard. Alone. In front of the mirror. For hours. Until I got it right. If I made one tiny mistake, I started it over. I memorized every last detail until I didn't forget anything. It was like binge studying for a test so that I could write every answer perfectly. Although I became frustrated and disgusted with myself as I watched how I moved in front of the mirror, and although I had to repeat some of the dance steps over and over and over again, I slowly started feeling more confident in my ability.

My dance team got our costume for Blue and Gold, and because we were doing Madonna's "Holiday," we were all dressed in different party-like colors. Mine was pink. At the end of the dance, we were to grab little party ribbons out of our front pockets. By this time, my dancing had gotten better. Not substantially better, but at least I wasn't terrible anymore.

*　　*　　*

As Blue and Gold got closer, Savannah was really getting on my nerves. I thought she could say the most ridiculous things. For example, my brother told me she'd called our house phone asking for me but that he'd told her I wasn't home. He said that, before she hung up, she muttered a nasty name to him.

I became angry hearing she'd said that, so I called her and asked if she'd done what my brother had said. "No," she replied, apparently fuming, "and I can't believe you would accuse me of something like that." After a minute or two of listening to her blabbering, I hung up the phone.

The phone rang. I picked up. "I can't believe you hung up on me!" There was a part of me that was relieved she would call back after being hung up on. It was an indication that I meant enough to her for her to call me back. I felt more respect for her, closer to her even—at least in that moment—and felt a little guilty for hanging up.

The next day, I walked into Spanish class and saw Savannah sitting at her desk looking depressed. I sat down in front of her.

She looked at me. "Why did you…How could you…?" She talked at me and questioned me for a few minutes longer. My sense was that she had a right to feel upset. I had done and said things without thinking of her feelings, and I had acted upon my impulses without considering anything else.

The next argument we had was about her not wanting to sit in the audience at the Blue and Gold performance. I was very hurt when she said she wasn't coming. After our heated discussion, I decided to give her the silent treatment.

During science class, Savannah went up to Ms. Robertson's desk to get something. On the way back to her seat, she placed a note on my desk. It started out with, *What's your problem?* Then it went into reminding me she had already apologized for not being able to come and why she wasn't able to be there.

There was a part of me, in my gut, that knew she was right—I knew I was overreacting. Regardless, I still had a desire to throw some sort of temper tantrum like a two-year-old kid. But there was still a part of me that was hurt she wasn't coming. I was angry that she wasn't taking Blue and Gold seriously. That was when I realized how much her presence there meant to me.

We didn't speak for a little while after that. Savannah began to sit on the opposite side of the classroom in Spanish, rather than next to me, since we weren't speaking anymore. Instead, Savannah sat with an acquaintance of ours. I noticed the student looking at me, and then looking at Savannah before talking and whispering between themselves.

I figured she knew what was going on. I felt betrayed. It was as though this other student was now on Savannah's side, not mine. She probably thought I'd said too many bad things about Savannah and that I was mean and wrong. She probably felt bad for Savannah, too. Either way, I was the one left in the wrong.

Chapter 5

Artwork was plastered all over the first-floor hallway walls of the school building. The blue team's artwork was on one side of the hallway and gold's artwork was on the other. One piece of work was a letter written "from Madonna," congratulating us and wishing our blue team luck. When I first spotted it, I thought it really was from Madonna. Then I realized that of course it wasn't.

It was kind of scary lingering in the halls while we waited for the show to start. My palms were sweating and my knees were trembling. Oh, God, I hope I get this right, I kept thinking. I mean, I barely had the dance figured out. I went back through the routine itself and the way I would do the steps over and over in my head. In reality, I was only just learning to be a decent dancer.

As the show started, the "introduction" was a group of girls performing a dance routine for each team. When that was finished, each team would walk in. There was a noisy audience in the bleachers, with family, friends, and schoolmates rooting for the blue team on one side of the gym while the other side was filled with supporters for the gold team.

The judges, four of them, sat in chairs on the stage like kings and queens. They'd score each performance for the two nights— Thursday and Friday—and then total up the scores to decide a winner.

As the aerobics teams worked through their performances, I

felt like the gold team was better.

Next, it was our turn. I was terrified. The two lines of girls that had been patiently waiting in the hallway began to file in through the two doors at the back of the auditorium. Dressed in our "party colors," we all danced into the room to "Holiday" blasting at full volume. The blue side of the auditorium loved our entrance and cheered like crazy.

I was nervous, but I did have the steps. I got them all right on a basic level, but I barely moved my body at all, let alone with the right rhythm. During one of the dance steps, I felt particularly uncomfortable and knew I looked stupid. I swore I heard people in the audience laugh.

At the end of the dance, an almighty *BOOM* from the music signaled our final move. We all grabbed the curled ribbons out of our costume pockets and held them up in the air with one hand while our other hands fixed on our hips. Everyone loved it. My heart was hammering against my chest.

The gold team's dance went next. Their dance steps and moves were strong and tight. In fact, the whole routine looked pretty good. People were even singing along to the music as they danced. I remained quiet because that was the first time I'd ever heard the song from the *Flashdance* soundtrack.

I watched the gymnastics routines in awe. The blue team gymnasts, in particular, were fabulous. The races concluded the evening's competition. As a highly entertaining finale, I looked on in hysterics as the two teams of girls competed in mini races on scooters and skateboards among many other things.

At the end of the night, the judges totaled their scores. Sadly, although perhaps not surprisingly, our dance team lost. As it turned out, the blue team lost as a whole.

The next evening, Friday, was the final Blue and Gold night

when everyone had to do the whole thing all over again.

I was sitting on the floor with my dance team when the assistant principal announced the winners for that second night. "Ladies and gentlemen, the winner of tonight's dance competition is..." She paused for what seemed like an eternity. "The blue team!"

The first thing I saw was Patty and her little helpers jump to their feet, screaming at the top of their voices while bouncing around and hugging one another. They were acting like they'd just won the lottery. But I was cheering too. I was happy. And surprised.

More of the blue teams were announced as the Friday winners, including the amazing gymnastics team. The blue team was crowned the winner for Friday night.

The assistant principal went on to announce the winners for each team for both nights totaled. Most of the teams announced were blue.

When the time came to announce the overall winner for the dance competition, it was the blue team's name that was called out. All of the girls on my team, including me, went absolutely crazy. I was so thrilled. I couldn't believe I won the first dance competition I'd ever entered. The whole experience had wound up being rewarding and gave a much-needed boost to my confidence.

To finish off the competition, the blue team was announced as the winner for Blue and Gold, 1989. I was absolutely ecstatic.

*　　*　　*

After the performance, the teacher in charge of our dance team approached me with a big smile on her face. "I was so proud of you, Mary, just getting so into it," she said, patting me on my shoulder.

One part of me felt good hearing this. Another part of me felt not so good—it was a reminder that while I'd gotten good, at one point I'd been horrendously bad.

As my parents drove me home that night, my father talked about the show. He sounded proud of me. He said, "At first, when I saw the gold team's dance, I was like, 'Oh no, they'll never beat that.' Then, when I saw your dance, I thought, well, maybe…" It seemed like he'd been really into it. My mother didn't seem quite as enthusiastic, but I sensed she was happy.

Me, I was in the car just looking out the window and daydreaming about the past two days. Blue and Gold was over for the year but, from then on, I truly was a Blue and Gold girl. I became a big Stella Maris High School fanatic in general, despite the bullying I got, and I became more interested in various extracurricular activities.

*   *   *

The Regents exams were coming up, so I started putting more effort into studying as hard as I could at every opportunity. But I just couldn't get it. Academically, I continued to suffer.

I tried to no end to focus on the upcoming Regents. I took a million practice tests. Failed them all. Seeing my struggles, my father helped me with some of them. When he explained the subject matter to me, it made sense. However, it was the test itself, the exam questions, that really got to me. There was something about the Regents exams and Regents classes that just didn't work for me, yet I always blamed myself. What was wrong with me?

I was spending slightly less time totally spiking my hair up. Instead, I was trying to highlight my natural curls by blow-drying them and then spiking up my bangs. I still had no idea what I was doing, but I was obsessed with looking really good.

In classes, I'd frequently ask to go to the bathroom so I could check my hair in the mirror. I guess it got figured out that was the reason I was constantly going to the bathroom. When I asked to go one time in Spanish class, the teacher said no. But then smiled and said, "Your hair looks lovely." Savannah, who was sat behind me at the time, burst into laughter.

My bangs looked hideous. That's why people laughed. More and more people in school were picking on me, including girls in my homeroom. Cathy was even talking about not coming back next year.

Savannah had mentioned something about a girl who was apparently bothering her a lot lately. Her name was Britney Anderson. Even her name sounded really mean. Fortunately, I didn't really see Britney around.

The year was finally coming to an end. On the last day of math class, Sr. Helena announced to the class, "The only one who failed is my friend over there." Her finger was pointing at me. A few students murmured. I was in shock.

Everyone in class had signed a thank you card to give to Sr. Helena. My comment was, *I'll miss you, even though you always picked on me*. I meant it as a joke. I didn't know what else to say to her. Sr. Helena read all the comments on the card out loud. When she read mine, everyone laughed. One girl commented when she signed my freshman yearbook, *I'm glad you told Sr. Helena off!*

It turned out I still had a chance to pass math class; that was, if I passed the Regents exam. Basically, if a student passed the Regents, they passed the class. If anyone failed both the class and the Regents exam, they had to go to summer school and re-take the Regents in mid-August. If we passed the class but failed the Regents, we had the option of going to summer school in order to prepare to re-take the mandatory Regents in mid-August.

After I took the math Regents exam, I received a phone call from Sr. Helena and she told me I'd failed the Regents. She reminded me that I'd also failed the class. "So you definitely have to go to summer school," she said.

I was so shocked it was like the world stood still. I could not believe I had to go to summer school. It was like a death sentence. Summer school symbolized being stupid, unworthy of a pass, not to mention a ruined summer. It was the ultimate sign that I was indeed a failure, which sent me spiraling right back into my depression.

Savannah also ended up failing the math Regents. She hadn't failed the class, so she wasn't required to go to summer school, but I found out she was going to be going anyway because her parents were making her go.

By this time, Savannah and I were becoming close with a short sophomore named Diane. She lived in Howard Beach. I was fascinated by the fact that we now had a friend to hang out with who lived in the town where one of the most significant racial incidents of the decade had taken place.

Savannah pointed out to me the pizzeria where it had happened. We actually ate there a couple of times, too. I felt funny and a little scared whenever I was in the vicinity. And people I knew, girls in my classes, were associated with this very location. Either their family member was a part of it or they most likely knew the guys who did it.

Savannah, and particularly her sister and mother, were not afraid to admit their prejudice against African American people. The same could be said for a lot of people at Stella. I, on the other hand, was strongly against any kind of racial prejudice. My parents, particularly my father, had passionately instilled anti-racism against African Americans in me.

Unfortunately, I felt I had to be hush-hush about that around some of my friends both in and out of school. Sometimes, I'd even pretend to agree with their racism in fear of being turned on if I spoke out. But I thought their comments and their attitude toward the whole thing was horrific. It was interesting how the racist comments were never said to minority students' faces, only ever behind their backs. These racist girls were actually pretty scared of the African Americans, so it was just tough shit that they talked.

*   *   *

Summer school was starting, and I dreaded it. It turned out that Stella girls were not the only ones attending Stella for summer school. Other students, including real-life boys from other schools, were also coming to Stella for the summer.

Savannah and I were going to be in the same math class, which I was glad about. Sr. Dolores, who was the other instructor of math besides Sr. Helena, was going to be teaching our class. I was glad about this, too. Everyone had heard that, compared to Sr. Helena, Sr. Dolores was a very good teacher. I knew nothing about her, but I was still scared. Because I'd done so poorly in math that year, I couldn't see how I was going to miraculously get it in six weeks. But I was determined to try.

Sr. Dolores took attendance and called my name. She looked at me and said, matter-of-factly, "Do you know why you failed, Mary? Because you had so many absences." Without another word about my failure, she continued down the roster.

I didn't know what she meant exactly, but she shed new light on my problem. Was she saying that I might have passed if it weren't for all my absences? Was she saying that if I'd made all the classes, I could have understood the material more? Maybe the problem wasn't my intelligence after all.

I surveyed the room and spotted a couple of faces I recognized. There was a very quiet girl, Bella. There was also another girl, Kate, who started talking to me and Savannah a lot. We really liked her and had a great time with her. She was pretty and funny and a blast to be around. Savannah started chatting with Bella here and there and told me at one point she thought she was kind of cool. I was surprised but decided to keep it in mind.

I paid close attention in every single class and did all my homework to the best of my ability. I didn't miss any days in summer school. Despite my improved attitude toward math, Savannah and I still did our fair share of fooling around in class. Whenever we got caught, Sr. Dolores would get on us about our behavior, but she wouldn't shame us or punish us like Sr. Helena used to.

Much to my surprise, I had a great time in summer school.

My birthday was in August, and I was going to be in school. That was a first. Originally, I'd dreaded having to spend my birthday in school, but now I was really thrilled. People in school had become my main social life.

I got a few balloons from Savannah and even from a couple of other people, too. I was so happy that I wrote on the blackboard that Savannah and I would be best friends forever.

When Sr. Dolores came in, she guessed it was me who wrote on the board and ordered me to go wash it off. After filling up a bucket with water and finding a sponge, I returned to the classroom and found everyone was staring at me, laughing. As I looked at Sr. Dolores, she said, "Get your white hands in there!" Everyone was hysterical. I had to wash the board in long vertical stripes. Savannah and Bella mimicked, "Get your white hands in there!" for the rest of the afternoon.

The one and only morning I was sitting in class early, a tall girl with straight black hair appeared in the doorway. She said something to Savannah, which I assumed wasn't anything nice by the look on Savannah's face, and then she whipped her hair round over her shoulder and left.

Savannah told me it was Britney Anderson—her new "enemy"—the incredibly mean girl who kept picking on her. That was the first time I'd ever seen Britney in the flesh. She was only in the doorway for a couple of seconds, so I didn't know what to think. From the way Savannah made her sound, Britney was very scary. But, oh well, I never saw Britney around and she wasn't picking on me. I didn't ever plan on doing or saying anything to get her to pick on me, so I was good.

Much to everyone's surprise, I was doing really well in math. As my grades improved, I became even more furious at Sr. Helena, my former math teacher. Mental block in math, indeed. I had a mental block with her, I guess. She sucked. Now I knew it wasn't my fault.

However, despite taking a bunch of practice tests and scoring really high on all of them, when I took the summer Regents in August, I still scored on the low side. I did manage to pass, which of course was what mattered the most, but I couldn't help feeling disappointed because I had gotten all those high scores all summer and had really felt like I knew what I was doing. Still, I had a lot more confidence in myself and felt I had some closure over what had traumatized me academically in math freshman year.

Chapter 6

With the Regents exams over, I had the middle of August to relax. I saw Christy and her cousin around my neighborhood occasionally. They would laugh at me whenever I passed them, and I tortured myself with endless questions. What happened? What did I do?

One day in the summer, Savannah, her sister Jetta, and I were hanging out at Forest Park. I was still feeling angry at Christy for the way she was treating me, so we went to a pay-phone and prank-called her house. Savannah made the call. I didn't hear what Savannah said, but Christy's mother had answered the phone.

A few minutes later, still hanging out near the phone, we saw a station wagon driving by. It was Christy's mother. As the car passed, Christy's mother looked back at me. "Call my house again, and you're dead!" she screamed out of the window.

I saw Christy's smug face in the car, too. She was sitting in the backseat, staring at me through narrowed eyes.

As a reflex, I shouted, "Fuck you!" I really didn't know what else to say.

Really, I was thinking, oh shit, we shouldn't have done that. I'm so stupid. I prank-called them from a pay phone right near their house? How stupid could I be? And it was childish.

Not long after this, I got a call at my house. When I picked up, I could hear giggling. I asked who it was, and a girl said, "Melissa." I suspected it was either Christy or her cousin, but I wasn't sure.

"Melissa who?" I asked.

"Melissa Mars," the voice replied, followed by more giggling. I hung up. Well, I had that coming. I'd done it first.

Soon after the prank call incident, one of my childhood friends, Ellen, came to visit me. As we chatted in the park near my house on the swings, Christy and her cousin entered the park. Fear immediately consumed me. I wasn't sure if they were going to come up to me or not, but I knew the chances of them doing exactly that were pretty good.

Ellen and I stayed on the swings as they walked toward us. Christy then ran ahead of her cousin and stood behind the fence in front of the swings.

"Do you have a fucking problem?" she said to me, smirking.

My hands trembled against the chains of the swing. I tried to block out most of what she said as she started snapping at me, listing things I'd said and done. The only one I heard was, "You told my mother to go fuck herself."

After she finally stopped yelling, I started pleading with her. I finished with, in a rather shaky and desperate voice, "I never wanted to have a problem with you."

Christy looked at her cousin, who smirked back at Christy. She then yelled another thing I managed to block out, I think it was a threat, before they both turned on their heel and left. I felt so humiliated this happened in front of Ellen.

At another point during the summer, I was walking with Savannah in her neighborhood, Ozone Park. A car passed us by and Christy's cousin hung her head out the window. She, too, lived in Ozone Park.

She looked right at me and yelled, "Slut!" before the car continued to drive away.

*   *   *

Despite my problems with the girls, men seemed to be fawning all over me. I was traveling on the bus to Savannah's house one afternoon. A man in the seat in front of me had a cowboy hat on. He turned around in his seat and stared at my chest—I actually had one by that point. He wouldn't stop. He didn't turn his head away. I felt violated. Quick, I thought, think of something to say.

"Do you have a problem?" I snapped at him.

He smiled, shook his head, and turned around. I was proud of myself for having thought of something good to say instead of just taking shit. But I still obsessed about what I did. Was it me? The outfit I was wearing? My face? My hair?

It had been one strange summer.

Chapter 7

Sophomore Year

This year, I was getting the sense that Christy might initiate a fight with me. I'd never fought anyone before, so I was pretty freaked out by the idea it might actually happen.

As I walked around one night with Rebecca, my friend from elementary school, I asked her about how to fight someone.

Rebecca said, "You can use your nails. If you have keys, you can use those. You can pull her hair." I soon realized that fighting didn't have to be about turning into Rocky Balboa and punching my way to victory. I had no idea how to punch, but I was sure I could handle the other stuff Rebecca was talking about—I'd just go for it.

One Saturday night, Savannah, Jetta, and I took a walk in my neighborhood. It was dark and I couldn't see so well, but as we walked by Christy's house, I know we stayed across the other side of the street.

When I heard two girls laughing, I knew the laughter was targeted at us.

"Hey, Mary Carol Powell...Hey, Mary Carol Powell," they chanted, followed by more laughter.

Sometimes, people made fun of my full name because it sounded silly. Actually, Mary Carol was my birth name, but people started calling me Mary when I was twelve.

Then I heard Christy's mother yell something to me from the house, so I shot something back at her from across the street. As

Savannah, Jetta, and I reached the avenue and continued to walk further down the block, I heard a loud "Hey!" from way back behind us.

We turned and saw three girls running toward us at full speed. It was Christy, her cousin Judy, and a girl who was mine and Christy's classmate in junior high. This was the first time I'd seen her since eighth grade graduation.

While the three girls closed in on us, Christy yelled at me for saying something to her mother. I started marching away from her with Savannah and Jetta close behind me. "You told my mother to go fuck herself!" Christy yelled.

As I turned to reply, I found Christy within inches of my face. She challenged me and shoved me backwards. I immediately dove at her shoulders to return the shove. Before I knew what was happening, we were both going at it. I grabbed a handful of her hair and we swiped and clawed at each other.

As we fought, I overheard Savannah say, "I'm not intervening!"

One of Christy's girls responded, "You do and I'll kick your ass!"

Christy's fist hit my face, but it didn't hurt as much as when our heads accidentally bumped together.

I finally tore myself away from her grasp and started stomping away in the opposite direction, Savannah and Jetta behind me once again. The three girls were still hot on our heels.

"Christy, I don't want to fight you!" I said. I was no longer scared of her, but I didn't want to do this. It was wrong. I didn't want to hurt her. We used to be friends!

"Well, I don't want to fight you either!" She was smirking. If she didn't want to fight me, what was she doing?

Christy's parents then appeared behind her, arms folded across their chests. They sent Christy and the other two girls home, then Savannah and Jetta took off to go back to my house.

Christy's father grabbed me by the arm and yelled in my face as I tried to get away from him. He dragged me over to Christy's mother, who screamed at me and called me a little slut.

He said to his wife, "Smack her, smack her!"

A fresh wave of terror boiled in my stomach as I noticed her angry stare. I was scared of her hitting me. Perhaps she saw the frightened and pleading look on my face because she just glared at me and said, "No, I won't waste my time with her."

Christy's father grabbed my arms again and said he was taking me home. I started to cry, pleading with him to stop and let me go, but he didn't.

As we neared the front steps of my house, I was relieved to be back home. I realized how wrong Christy's father was to manhandle me like that, and I was quite sure my parents would take my side. I jerked my arm away from his grasp and stomped up the stairs to my house.

When I got inside, I found my father and started to explain about what had happened, anger oozing out of every pore of my skin. Savannah and Jetta were sitting on the living room couches and backed up my story about what had happened, adding in their own complaints about the event.

My father held his hand up in front of my face and told me to be quiet. When I ignored his request and continued with my version of the story, he glared at me with rage and warned, "Mary Carol, do you want me to hit you in front of your friends?"

When I protested, he repeated in a louder voice, "Mary Carol, do you want me to hit you in front of your friends?" I was scared of him and what his anger might turn in to. Why would he do this? I hated him. Normally, I would continue to fight him back regardless of the consequences. He had hit me many times before, but I had always fought back. Still, I was embarrassed and didn't want to create a scene in front of Savannah and Jetta.

Savannah and Jetta were quiet. The phrase "Mary Carol, do you want me to hit you in front of your friends?" became one of their favorite ways to tease me for several days afterwards.

Before I had another chance to get my father on my side, Christy's father burst through the front door of my house and began to lecture me about my behavior in front of everyone. "Is this the way Christians are supposed to behave? Is this the love of Jesus?" I hated him for his warped version of what had really happened.

It turned out that Christy's parents and my parents scheduled a "meeting" for the next day, which was to include a discussion between Christy, myself, my parents, and her parents. The meeting wasn't something I was ever invited to—my presence was demanded. I didn't have a choice.

The next morning, Savannah and I spent the train ride telling Bella all about what happened. When Bella heard about the meeting, she said, "You guys are going to make up and be friends again."

No way. Christy hated me. "I sincerely doubt it," I replied, shaking my head.

Bella laughed. "I'm telling you, you will."

Savannah added, "Yeah, you watch, they'll be best friends again after their meeting."

Their words of encouragement actually made me feel better. The idea of making up with Christy made me happy, but realistically, I thought it was impossible.

That night, mine and Christy's parents, along with Christy and I, sat at the table in their dimly lit dining room. Christy sat on one side of the table diagonally opposite from me on the other side. She wasn't looking at me. I glanced at her a couple of times, nervous and scared.

Our parents talked, both to each other and to us. I didn't listen to what they said. My mind was too busy thinking everything over. I realized that Christy was doing to me what I'd once seen her do about a year before. She'd yelled at two girls she didn't like in the class under us in junior high; she'd called them "sluts."

She seemed so cruel and scary. It was like she was this sweet, reserved, and quiet little thing, unless you got on her bad side, then she was like someone in the mafia. And now, she was targeting me. But what had I done? I concluded it was because she'd realized I was a dork. She'd heard from her cousin how I was seen as a dork at Stella; that was it.

One thing that was brought up in the meeting was the prank call. I denied I'd done it. Christy's mother said she believed me and admitted that it hadn't even sounded like me. Well, only I knew that was because it wasn't me. It was actually Savannah who'd called.

Christy's mother said to me, "Mary, if you didn't make the call, I'm sorry. I apologize." I appreciated her apology, and I felt really bad. I was so ashamed to admit we had indeed prank called her.

At one point, I shot Christy a quick glance. She was still looking down and her eyes were red with tears. I also felt like I was going to cry. I wanted us to talk and be friends again.

After our parents had talked—I guess, to their satisfaction— they became quiet. Christy's father joked, "You two can look at each other now." Christy and I looked at each other and laughed silently. I felt better. Our parents left the room and we were alone.

At first, Christy and I sat quietly at the table, neither of us wanting to be the first to speak. After a minute or so of awkward silence, I apologized, and she did too. But I don't think she was as interested in making up as I was. I still wanted to connect with her somehow, but then I remembered Christy's cousin and I suddenly felt scared. Christy was here, but her cousin wasn't. I'd still have to see her cousin on the streets and at Stella, right? I asked Christy, "Is she mad, your cousin?"

Christy was looking away. She said quietly, "No."

We got to talking about when I'd seen them at Blue and Gold, and she said she'd seen me dance.

"You were good," she said. Those three words made me feel awesome.

By the end of the night, I was on a high. We'd made up. It was over. As my parents and I walked home and rounded the corner toward our house, I smiled and thought, Bella and Savannah had been right! I couldn't believe it.

*   *   *

Cathy had come good on her threats to leave after freshman year and had transferred to another school for sophomore year. We never had any contact with her again, not even so much as a phone call.

At lunch table this year were Caitlin—the girl who'd congratulated me for telling Sr. Helena off—her friends Lucy—the one who'd had the nerve to get the math problem correct in class— Jan, Savannah, and Bella. Kate from summer school sat with us for some time as well. Not long after sophomore year began, Kate cut herself off from us completely. Not only did it hurt me, but it was also insulting because I knew why she'd left us. We were too dorky or whatever for her type, so of course she'd be bored. In a sense, I didn't blame her. She was out of our league.

By that time, I was much more hyper and louder than my friends were. In response, they would often tease me about it, usually affectionately.

Some of us, especially me, were becoming obsessed with the

band New Kids on the Block. It started back in freshman year when Rebecca, the old friend of mine from elementary school, had walked home with me one night and we went back to her apartment. She showed me a magazine filled with music stars, and there was an article and photos of a group called New Kids on the Block. I'd heard a couple of their songs.

"They're so cute!" Rebecca exclaimed as she drooled over the magazine. I looked at this photo and saw some really fucking hot guys. They looked like they were in their late teens. One of them, Jordan, was the most gorgeous to me. He had black wavy hair and a long skinny braid that probably went all the way down his back. Wow. I'd decided he was my favorite.

Later though, I changed to Donnie. Caitlin was practically in love with Joe, the youngest band member, but Savannah favored the brothers, Jordan and Jon. We would spend hours debating over who was the cutest while Bella simply rolled her eyes and made fun of the entire band. In a way that would make us laugh.

Lunch was, for the most part, always fun. We usually had a lot of laughs. For me, it was a great way to release the stress I'd built up over the morning. Lunch, and any other time spent with my friends at school, lifted my mood. I came to find that I was a happy, spirited person whose friends meant a lot to her.

Sometimes, however, the fun would go too far. There were times when my hyperactivity proved inappropriate, and there were other times when I kind of acted like a kid. During lunch period one day, I was in the hallway being scolded by one of the nuns about something. Before she'd even finished, I ran away from her, crying with laughter. I raced to our table shouting, "Hide me! Hide me!" before I climbed under the table and hid as best I could. Although I think some of my friends were amused by my antics, I had the sense some of them weren't. The nun found me crouched under the table, told me to get out, and then continued where she'd left off with her scolding.

*   *   *

I noticed around that time that Rebecca was often canceling our plans and not calling when she said she would. I never took it personally, but I found it very frustrating.

I felt like causing some drama and punishment for Rebecca, so I considered writing her a letter to end the friendship.

One morning in gym, I sat next to Caitlin on the bleachers. I wanted attention and drama, so I called upon my depression and mumbled to Caitlin about how I was upset and didn't know what to do. And, of course, I told her all about Rebecca.

"I might write her a letter ending the friendship. What do you think?"

She said she didn't know. She didn't really seem in the mood to talk to me at all.

In the end, I wrote Rebecca a letter telling her why we couldn't be friends anymore. Rebecca then called me on the telephone. "I just got your letter. I haven't read it yet," she said. I could tell from her voice that she was surprised and anxious, but not upset. I'd never done this before with her, or anyone else for that matter, so I could feel the drama starting to build.

I told her I couldn't talk because I was in the middle of something and hung up.

That was the last time we ever spoke. She never called me back. I figured she was probably hurt I'd done that to her, and admittedly, it caused me some guilt.

After re-thinking everything that had happened and what I'd done, I called her home and spoke briefly with her mother. When she asked for a message, I said, "Tell her it's Mary. I, um, I ended our friendship, but I want to talk to her...as soon as possible."

"Oh," Rebecca's mother said quietly. Her voice told me that the chances of Rebecca calling me back or wanting to bother with me again were very slim. I sensed it wasn't going to happen. And it never did.

Chapter 8

One friend I was really happy to have during sophomore year was Lana, my now junior friend, because she was pretty and cool. I was glad to be seen with her.

Once, I went out with her and a couple of her Italian friends. We all went to Manhattan to shop and hang out. I remember feeling shy and unable to talk a whole lot, but I was just glad to be seen with them, walking with them. At one point, a guy laughed in our direction. One of Lana's friends wondered aloud if he had been laughing at them.

Lana mumbled, "No, he wasn't laughing at you, he was laughing at..." I didn't hear what she said to finish the sentence, but I was positive that it was me the guy had laughed at. I was also pretty sure Lana and her friends knew it, too. Yet again, I was known to more people as "weird."

Caitlin was another girl I was really happy to be close with. I really liked her. I remember being on the phone with her one time. She was talking about future plans for her life and mentioned to me at one point, "If we're still close friends..." It made me feel excited because it was a confirmation that she was a close friend.

I was thrilled to be making all these close friends, who were also pretty cool, outside of Savannah. Freshman year had been all about Savannah, but I thought these new friends were cooler and much more supportive of me than she ever was.

By that time, I really wanted a boyfriend. One afternoon, my father and brothers decided to play ball in a park near the mall. I don't remember why, but I was with them. As I sat in nearby benches on the concrete field and watched them play—not the game, I never cared for sports—I had many thoughts going through my mind.

Then, I noticed a group of guys hanging out on the field. One of them looked so cute. I couldn't believe my eyes when I saw him. I decided I must, *must* have him as a boyfriend. Turning my head toward and away from him several times, I wanted to make it obvious that I was looking at him so he'd come over to talk to me. It was a simple enough plan, but I was dying with nerves; I was scared.

Much to my surprise, it worked. He came over and talked to me. He asked my name, we made small talk, and he told me his name was Charles. His friends kept looking over at us and laughing, but they soon lost interest and decided to carry on playing ball.

Before we left, Charles gave me his phone number. Both of us were equally as excited about the unexpected meeting. He was so handsome! Even better, he might now be my boyfriend!

The next evening, I sat alone on my brother's bed when I decided to call Charles. He picked up, and I could hear a couple of his friends talking and laughing in the background. Before we'd had a chance to exchange more than a few words, one of his friends grabbed the phone and took over Charles' side of the conversation. "Hey, Mary? Charles wants to know if you want to make love to him," he said, laughing.

I couldn't believe what he just said. Eeew! Make love to him? Wasn't that what married people did? Just the thought of it freaked me out. It was so gross.

I think I responded, "Uh, no." Yet I stayed on the phone. I really liked this guy, so I cradled the phone to my ear and tried to brush off what just happened.

Charles came back to the phone and mumbled an apology for his friend's interruption. Before ending the call, we made plans for us all to meet at the mall that Friday night. Deciding I didn't want to go alone, I invited a friend from my old junior high school to come with me. I was too scared to be on my own. After all, I'd never been on any kind of date before.

Friday night arrived, and we took the bus from my house to its stop outside the mall. As soon as we stepped inside the mall, I saw two of Charles' friends hanging out and talking between themselves. We went over to them and I asked where Charles was. They said he wasn't with them and wasn't coming. I told them thanks and turned to my friend. "Let's go," I said, flooded with disappointment.

"Mary, is that what we came all the way down here for? To say *hi*?" She started criticizing me like crazy. I felt embarrassed. I'd proved, right in front of her, that I didn't know how to talk to guys. Shy little Mary. She immediately added my failures of the day to her list of past insults about me and my useless personality.

I insisted that I would call Charles when I got home and tried to drum into her how I knew there was still hope. My friend wasn't convinced.

I tried calling Charles a few times after that, but he never called back. I was beyond disappointed, and I obviously took it personally. How could I not?

*   *   *

Stella announced they were hosting a dance. They hadn't done that the previous year. We were excited because, for this dance, guys were coming from other schools. *Finally!* Needless to say, I got really dressed up.

Most of the start of the night was spent looking for really cute guys. Eventually, Savannah and I found one. He was adorable, and it didn't take much persuading to get him to dance with us. After a ton of encouragement from Savannah to convince me to dance with him, I agreed, but I was scared. Slowly, I started getting into the dancing and even did a spinning move my sister had taught me.

The cute guy said to me, "You're a really good dancer."

I was surprised but so glad to hear that. It was another example for me of going from an F to an A.

A couple of New Kids on the Block songs came on. I found it quite weird how a lot of girls in my school didn't like them even though virtually every other girl in the world did. When one of their slow songs came on, I was on the dance floor with Savannah and the cute guy we'd met. Me and Savannah were joking around in front of him and she was teasing me about me possibly slow-dancing with him.

Before I had a chance to argue, he took me in his arms and said, "Alright!" and started slow-dancing with me. Oh, fuck, I thought. I'd never slow-danced with a guy before, never been in a guy's arms before, and yet that was what I'd been wanting—to do exactly that. Actually, despite my fears, it was a really fun experience.

Savannah was happily giggling away to herself as she watched us floating around the dance floor. After the slow song had finished, the three of us went outside to the back of the school to hang out for a while. As he was talking under the glow of natural moonlight rather than artificial disco lights, I looked at him more closely and saw that he wasn't as handsome as I'd first thought. I wasn't crazy about his nose. I wanted to have someone absolutely gorgeous, with virtually no flaws.

He gave me his number, and we hung around outside the school alone together for a little bit. I decided that because of his "flaws," I wouldn't pursue it any further.

I spent a lot of time thinking of who I could dig up around my neighborhood as a boyfriend. Maybe a guy I'd gone to junior high with. As I remembered this guy, Frankie, it hit me that he'd always been kind of cute, but I was hearing around that he'd now gotten really cute. What sealed the deal for me was that I heard he looked somewhat like Joe McIntyre from New Kids on the Block. It was settled. Frankie it was.

*   *   *

My junior high school was having some sort of talent show one night, and I decided to go with my sister, who was in sixth grade there at the time. Plus, I was hoping Frankie would be there, of course. Indeed, he was there, and he was all I could think about the whole time I was sitting in the dark auditorium.

I did eventually get to see Frankie at the talent show. He looked really cute, even cuter than I'd remembered. I got one of my sister's friends to tell him I liked him.

I waited nervously for her to return. Suddenly, I heard a bunch of guys exclaim, "Oooohhhh!" Then laughter, lots of it.

My sister's friend came back with a reluctant look on her face. She said Frankie had said something really bad.

"He said, 'Only when she shaves her beard, takes a shower, and washes her hair...only then I might let her lick my balls.'"

I felt like a huge stone had barreled into my stomach. I was so insulted and humiliated. Not only had the guy I liked turned me down, but he'd also laughed it off and insulted me horribly, using the exact same comments people had made in school.

Maybe things hadn't changed? Maybe I was still seen the same way? People used to think and say I was dirty. I didn't know why; I showered every day. I guessed it was the way I looked or the way I did my hair.

I certainly didn't wash my hair every single day, it was more like every other day because I thought that was all it needed. I thought I styled it well, considering I really didn't know how to do it properly. Really, I didn't know what else to do with it, and my mother hadn't exactly taught me anything about beauty or how to look after my appearance. I'd had to try to figure it out for myself by looking at people on the TV and in magazines, for example, but without someone helping me, I couldn't really do it right. Anytime a friend tried to "help," their attempts were punctuated with criticism and insults so I could barely follow their instructions, no matter how hard I tried.

The "beard" thing was most likely my side burns, which was especially humiliating to hear because I was so self-conscious about them to begin with. I'd never had any idea why I had them in the first place.

Somehow, though, for whatever reason, I felt confident enough to go tell him off—very unlike me. I just felt so angry and hurt. I looked for him and found him outside the building, talking to a couple of other people.

I started yelling and cursing at him. He looked at me with surprise, then he tried to calm me down by saying he didn't know what I was talking about. "Let's go talk about this," he said. His attempts to calm me were so fake they made me laugh.

When his friends came to see what was going on, he yelled at them, "Leave me alone! Thanks to you, I'm in this predicament! You got me in this predicament!" Then I saw him smirk at his friends.

"Is this a fucking joke?" I screamed.

"No, no it's not a joke," he said as he led me to the grassy field of the school's rectory. We were alone in a quiet, dark corner between buildings. No one else was around.

I yelled at him about what he'd said, but he continued to deny it. As I became calmer, I told him that I liked him but still pressed him about what he'd said. Eventually, he admitted he'd said it. He offered me a hug. I became excited. Did he like me?

He wrapped his arms around me and then slid his hand over my rear end, albeit briefly.

"Stop," I said quietly, unable to understand why he'd just done that.

We made plans for him to come over to my house the next day after school. I was overflowing with excitement! Frankie was so cute. And he was going to be inside my house!

I was also confused. What was the whole "lick my balls" and patting my rear end all about? Was that supposed to be part of making out?

*   *   *

On the bus the next morning, I sat with Savannah. I wanted to tell her what happened. I still felt humiliated about the words he'd used when he insulted me behind my back and I was embarrassed to repeat them, but I figured, well, Savannah's my friend, I *have* to tell her. It was such a big part of the story, so it's not like I could just leave it out. I told her everything.

Savannah laughed about what he'd said. She thought it was funny. I guessed she had a right to laugh, so I just took it in my stride and went along with it.

During Spanish class, while I was musing over my crush on Frankie and reveling in how happy and excited I was about him, I wrote *Frankie and Mary* on my notebook with a huge love heart in between the names. I might have a boyfriend now, I told myself.

That night after school, in spite of my daydreaming the entire day, Frankie didn't come to my house. He didn't show up. I felt disappointed and depressed, though a part of me wasn't surprised.

And that was it for Frankie. I was totally grossed out by him by that point, and I was partially thankful I didn't have his number to call him.

Chapter 9

A couple of months later, there was a dance at an all-boys school. There, Savannah and I met a guy named Andy. He was nice and okay-looking. He had a friend with him. We danced and talked with them for most of the night, and Andy and I even slow-danced several times. Again, I was nervous.

Toward the end of the night, the four of us hung out in the school hallway and talked some more. Andy was mostly talking to me, and his friend was mostly talking to Savannah. Andy told me he liked me and wanted to go out with me. I was so excited at the idea of going on an actual date, to actually have a boyfriend. I immediately said yes.

When we said goodnight after the dance, Andy gave me a quick kiss on the lips. And that was my first kiss.

I raved to Savannah about him kissing me on the lips and how I couldn't believe that just happened. Savannah was ambivalent about going out with his friend, but she had a feeling he liked her.

When we went to school the following Monday, word had gotten around that "Mary Powell *actually* danced with someone." It was so embarrassing. During homeroom, I told the girls I normally talked to all about it. I mentioned he was a year younger than me; he was a freshman.

As soon as Caitlin heard who it was, she opposed me going out with him. She said her friend, also a freshman in Stella, had gone out with him but had wound up hating him because he was so annoying and clingy. Caitlin repeated over and over again that I shouldn't go out with him. It totally rained on my parade. I was disappointed—again. I had been so excited about finally having a boyfriend.

I asked around about how the other freshman girl might react if she found out I was dating Andy. Caitlin warned, "They're going to make fun of you."

Her comment alone was enough to get me worried, and I started to doubt whether or not the Andy thing was a good idea. I also brought up the fact that he was fourteen—a year younger than me—and asked if that was weird or how it would make me look.

A student sitting next to me said, "That doesn't matter. Does he treat you good?"

I wanted to answer her question. I couldn't not answer her question. It was said in a tone where an automatic answer was obviously expected.

But I didn't know if he treated me good or not; I only just met him. He had so far, and he seemed like the type who would.

So I said, "Yeah."

"Then that's all that matters," the girl replied.

Still, I couldn't take her argument seriously. What Caitlin said had already really got to me.

Caitlin added, "He's got a lot of money. He'll buy you jewelry and things, but still..."

Well, that sounded nice. For a second, I reconsidered, but I couldn't date a guy just for that. If he had annoying qualities and was likely to smother me—especially if girls would be making fun of me for dating him the whole time—then I was not interested.

The freshman whom Andy had apparently dated, and whom I'd never met before, was the next to confront me about the issue. She said she'd heard I was going to go out with Andy. Feeling too scared to tell her the truth and wanting to avoid any fights, I told her I was going to dump him. She said she was glad, that he was possessive and clingy. She imitated the way he said, "How ya doing?" in a really funny way, with a lisp.

I wasn't sure if I was going to dump Andy. Nevertheless, Savannah and I went to the mall to meet him and his friend. I wanted Savannah to be there because I still didn't want to go alone; she knew I had huge hesitation. Plus, Andy's friend was interested in her.

When Savannah and I got to the mall, we saw Andy and his friend waiting by the front door. Andy kissed me on the lips with more enthusiasm than I'd expected, and not knowing what else I could do, I kissed him back. Then, he put his arm around my waist. I was so uncomfortable playing the "girlfriend" figure, but we all managed to hang out for a few hours without any other weird stuff happening.

The next day, I broke it off with him on the phone.

Savannah told me one of the popular girls had said to her, "I heard Mary Powell actually got a guy to dance with her."

The whole story really got around. Savannah and I walked past the gym one time, and Ms. Robertson was standing by the gym door. We stopped to say hi. "So I heard that you danced?" she asked through a mouthful of candy bar. Again, I felt humiliated. Everyone seemed to be making such a big deal over this. Why? It was because it was me, that's why. No one could believe I could get a guy. I was getting unfair attention. And it felt horrible.

*　　*　　*

It was my sister's twelfth birthday. She was having all her friends over, and I was having some of my friends over, too.

My sister's party guests turned out to be virtually her entire class. I couldn't believe how popular she was, especially being related to me. Of course, though, Andrea was totally adorable. She had a strong way of getting what she wanted from people, yet she was very funny and charming at the same time.

I felt proud that my own friends got to see that *my* sister was popular and had twenty-five kids over. My living room was packed, which stressed out my parents a bit because we'd just gotten new carpeting that looked awesome. With a houseful of party guests, I thought I looked good in front of my friends—I looked normal.

My sister Andrea evaluated my hair style and went on to criticize it, along with my mother, as though it were up for discussion. She said that I'd blow-dried it too long. My mother agreed.

"Your hair used to look good before you started blow-drying it too much. It looked like you had a spiral perm!" my sister exclaimed. Spiral perms were big at the time. My mother was the background audience of my sister's observations, chiming in at times in agreement.

I took in every word they said, really believing that I was inadequate and a "failure" at making myself look pretty. It was like getting a C with teachers lecturing me on why I should have gotten an A.

After a half-day at school, I went with my mother to my old elementary school. She had to visit Andrea's class and asked if I wanted to go with her, saying we could stay for Andrea's lunch period. She was the "lunch mother" assigned to chaperone the class that day.

When my mother and I walked into the sixth grade classroom, my sister marched up to me with an irritated, disgusted, and embarrassed look on her face. "Why are you here? What are you doing here?" she asked in a loud, angry whisper.

It was a slap in the face. Obviously, I was a dork even to my own sister and she was embarrassed in front of her friends. I felt rejected and insulted.

It turned out, however, that all her friends thought I looked great that day, including my hair, which they said looked like I had a spiral perm. Plus, they liked my personality. Andrea then seemed happier I'd come and was comfortable enough for me to be on display in front of her friends.

Andrea told me their compliments, but in a manner that said, "Wow, you're actually okay!" She said it in an evaluative way, like I'd finally passed a test after years of failures. Of course, at that time, I thought her acceptance was well-deserved.

My friends would complain about Andrea, calling her spoiled and saying she was unfair and mean to me. I wouldn't say anything, but I would feel offended. She was my sister, after all, and I did love her. Although I felt no one had the right to insult my family, except those in the family, deep down, I knew they were right. It was hard to admit that to myself when other people said it, mainly because it was a confirmation of my feelings and thoughts toward Andrea.

They were true but too hard to deal with, so I suppressed them. They only came up to the surface here and there.

Andrea later dumped Christy's sister, as well as several others in her class. She and her army of girls made fun of anyone who wasn't cool and trendy. If I were in Andrea's class, I definitely would have been a victim. My own sister's.

*　　*　　*

As much as I loved her, Savannah was beginning to annoy me more and more. A lot of people didn't like her, including people in our own group of friends. At times, I would be relieved to find out other people had similar feelings toward her so I could vent to them.

Once, I sat with Caitlin at her locker during a free period while people were in their classes. The hallway was empty. Caitlin used to dislike Donnie from New Kids on the Block, but now she liked him. We were both annoyed at Savannah, who would insult Donnie. "And if Savannah doesn't like Donnie she should just shut up," Caitlin said. "I mean, it's different when Bella does it because at least she makes it funny." Good. Caitlin just put into words exactly what I'd been feeling lately.

Technically, Savannah was still my best friend, so I kept our friendship going. We regularly talked on the phone and went to each other's houses most weekends.

Two other girls suddenly started hanging out with our friend, Bella. It was mostly on the train. For a while, they pretty much talked to Bella but not the rest of us. They were Jordan, the girl who had sat next to me in science during freshman year but who I never spoke with, and a girl named India.

They would often come around, laughing and talking and hanging out with Bella. They didn't seem very interested in getting to know me and Savannah, but very gradually, that began to change—particularly on Jordan's part. Most of the time on the train, Jordan and India would share a Walkman and listen to music, away from us, or they would be talking to Bella. They would often start to either laugh with or at me when I got loud and crazy.

*　　*　　*

One time, Savannah, Jordan, India, and I were in the backseat of Bella's father's car with Bella in the passenger seat. I started making the girls laugh by doing imitations of teachers and cursing. They rolled around on the backseat and couldn't stop laughing. I realized part of the reason they were laughing so hard was because Bella's father sat quietly in the driver's seat.

"Mary, shut up!" they told me.

"I'm sorry," I said to Bella's father, still laughing.

Then the girls started snickering again, but Bella stayed motionless in her seat, facing forward and shaking her head. But I knew she was amused. As crazy as they thought and said I was, I knew my friends got a kick out of me. I made otherwise unhappy girls laugh hard. I saw this as a good thing. And I was proud.

After Jordan, India, and Savannah had been dropped off, I said again, only half-seriously to Bella's father, "I am so sorry for cursing."

Bella smirked and put her hands over her face. Her father just kept driving.

As we drove, I asked, "Bella, do you like Savannah?" I wanted to turn her against Savannah.

Bella got quiet for a second and in an irritated, defensive voice said, "Of course I like Savannah...Savannah's my friend."

I felt stupid, and I quickly grasped for straws. I turned it back to me and explained how and why she sometimes got on my nerves. I'd made Savannah sound bad. When I'd finished, Bella remained silent. I felt ashamed, embarrassed, like I was being a mean person.

Bella told me later on, joking that her father's nickname for me was "El Papagayo," or parrot in Spanish, meaning, he thought I was a chatterbox.

Chapter 10

Sophomore year was much more enjoyable for me than freshman year had been. I was making many more friends and I was no longer shy or quiet, at least when I was with my group. In fact, I was now loud, charismatic, and funny—often to a fault. I knew I could overdo it, especially when I became hyperactive and impulsive in my actions and speech. My friends liked me a lot, but some of them had to put me in my place at times; they seemed to get frustrated and annoyed.

Regardless, it kept a smile on my face knowing that I was becoming more popular, even if it was just among my friends. It hit me at one particular moment when I was joking around with Savannah and Bella. We were on the train while it was standing still outside Rockaway Park, the last stop. The doors were open, and I was being loud and silly, trying to run away from them. Bella yelled to Savannah, "Get her! Get her!"

The way she said that made it sound like I stood out to them in our circle, like I was the leader of the pack. It felt amazing to be in this role. I sure as hell had never been at the top of the pecking order before. At that moment, I reflected on how hard I'd had to work for that pole position. I'd earned it. Although I'd had to force myself through blood, sweat, and tears to be social and funny at times, now it had finally paid off.

But, while sophomore year was starting to become more fun, it was also about to become very traumatic.

Around November time, Savannah told me that she got into something of an argument with Angelica, the "god," in her homeroom. Savannah wound up calling Angelica a nasty name, but it was in response to Angelica bothering Savannah and calling Savannah the same name first.

That same day, I was in the locker room changing from my gym clothes into my uniform when a very tall, skinny, angry-looking girl stomped over to me. She looked like the black-haired one who Savannah had warned me about. The one who had not yet picked on me. It was Britney Anderson.

"Are you friends with Savannah Hudson?" she yelled in an intimidating and threatening manner.

"Yes."

She was only a couple of feet away from me. Everyone in the locker room was watching. She raised her arm, pointed at me, and yelled, "You tell your friend Savannah Hudson that if she says one more thing to my friend Angelica..." She continued to scream but I blocked out the rest of her words.

I had never been this intimidated by a peer in my life. Until now, I had never really been near this Britney girl before, so her accusations really came out of the blue. It was unfair; I had nothing to do with this, so why was I the one getting hurt?

I didn't know what to do. I was scared, I wanted to protect myself, and I was annoyed by Savannah anyway. So I told Britney I would give her the warning.

"I will have her head on a platter!" she informed me loudly as she walked away.

I turned away in shock and continued to change my clothes. Behind me, a girl named Isabella from my homeroom, who was also friends with Angelica, asked me, "Who is this Savannah? And why is she bothering my friend Angelica?" Wow, Angelica really was a god.

I played along to protect myself. I needed to get the negative attention off me. "I don't know. I don't know what she said or why she would do that."

Isabella continued to change and said some negative things about Savannah, including, "She's probably jealous."

But Isabella seemed kind of cool to me. And, after all, I was still trying to make more friends, so Isabella and I started talking with each other more over the next few months. I knew that was quite a bitchy thing for me to do and that I was being a traitor to Savannah in the process, but I didn't listen to my conscience at the time.

It felt weird that I was associating with Isabella, because she was from the main popular crowd. Definitely a very new experience for me.

When Savannah found out that I was friendly with Isabella, she made it quite clear she didn't like it. I tried to reassure her that Isabella was okay, but she made a couple of bitter comments like, "So are you and Isabella going to be best friends?"

*   *   *

One day during lunch period, some girls came over to bother Savannah. I think it was because of what she'd said about Angelica. One of the girls was called Kate, our old friend from summer school. Savannah had predicted that Kate would leave us, and she was right. Kate was definitely no longer our friend.

Some of the girls took chairs and sat down at our table. I was standing off to the side. First, they taunted Savannah, and then Kate looked at some of my friends. She smiled at each of them. Kate seemed to assume that our friends didn't like Savannah either. When Kate smirked at my friend Caitlin, to my horror, Caitlin smirked back at her. To make matters worse, when Kate smirked at a couple of my other friends, they too smiled back at her.

Our friends had sold Savannah out, but I had a sense that they might just be protecting themselves. Perhaps they thought if they took sides with the popular girls, they wouldn't get bullied themselves.

Still, I felt betrayed. My friends knew that Savannah was my best friend, and yet they still went behind her back.

The guilt stuck around. Here I was, betraying Savannah, talking badly about her, and to the popular girls of all people. I told myself that perhaps Isabella was okay and not like the rest of the bitchy group.

Plus, I'd also done it because I was trying to protect myself. I feared that if I didn't go along with Isabella, I'd get targeted too.

Regardless of Isabella's acquaintanceship with me, Britney Anderson started to make fun of me. And in a really nasty and mean way. It was very intimidating. Savannah hadn't been kidding when she warned that Britney really was terrible. The worst bullying I'd ever gotten.

I tried to avoid Britney Anderson as much as possible. Sometimes, I was successful in avoiding her, but at least half the time, I wasn't. She was in my gym class and sometimes around on my lunch period too.

Around the end of the holidays, I'd gotten pretty good at avoiding her. Her verbal abuse became minimal, or only said in passing, which was easier for me to ignore. I wondered if it was because she'd heard I was friends with Isabella.

*   *   *

Report card time came. I hadn't done very well. For the first trimester's report card, the policy was for parents to come in on an evening to pick it up.

There ended up being a big misunderstanding that caused a problem between me, Savannah, and Ms. Robertson. It was all my fault. I'd told Savannah something negative that I thought Ms. Robertson might have said about her. Savannah took it straight to Ms. Robertson.

On report card night, I went into one of the classrooms just as one group of students and parents were coming out. I had my report card, complete with low grades. Savannah and her sister walked by me and boasted about their high grades. Savannah smirked and said, "What did you get, Mary...a D?"

This made me feel like crap because, yes, I'd gotten bad grades. It made me feel inferior. Despite my upset, I couldn't bring myself to answer them back.

Savannah and Jetta had made a couple of mean comments to me before, but I'd always taken it as playful. I might've criticized her from time to time, but my intention was to tease, not make her feel bad. One of Savannah's responses had been, "Well, at least I'm not dumb." It was strange because, at that time, I was kind of going through an identity crisis. Because I was tired of being a dork, the idea of being "dumb" actually appealed to me. So I just laughed.

Anyhow, on report card night, Savannah told me that Ms. Robertson was mad at me. So I went to Ms. Robertson's classroom. She was at her desk and the room was empty. I poked my head in and apologized for whatever it was I'd said to make her mad. I was really embarrassed. Ms. Robertson shamed me with a long lecture. It was something to do with how I'd made Savannah think Ms. Robertson was mad at her. As I stood in the doorway, Ms. Robertson stared angrily at me and said, "I love Savannah." I felt terrible because I really wanted Ms. Robertson to like me, too. She finished her lecture by criticizing me about the shape my life was in.

I didn't like being disliked, and I didn't like Savannah "winning" over me. Now I was determined to get Ms. Robertson, who I was really starting to admire, to love me just as she said she loved Savannah. I'd make her love me even more than she loved her precious Savannah. I would pass by Ms. Robertson daily and say hi. I'd also pass by her homeroom and her lab to look and see if she was there.

*   *   *

I was excited and happy about the upcoming Christmas show. For weeks before, I had practiced the dance until my legs could no longer hold me up. The morning of the show, I took the bus to Rockaway, got a seat in front, and started talking to a girl I knew. Soon, Isabella got on.

When Isabella started talking to me, I told her I was in the dance that day. She looked excited and said, "Oh, you are? I can't wait. I'm going to be going too, Mary!" I felt happy because she did seem to genuinely like me.

I was really nervous as I waited backstage. But, as soon as the curtains parted and the music came on, I remember doing the first steps of the routine to a cheering and clapping audience. It was great fun. Thankfully, all my practicing paid off and the show went really well.

Savannah and I went around to say Merry Christmas to a lot of people in school. I told Savannah, as casually as I could, that I wanted to say Merry Christmas to Ms. Robertson. Secretly, I had a card for her. I also wondered what she thought of how I danced. Maybe, since I danced pretty well, that would make her like me.

We went to knock at the faculty lounge door and Ms. Robertson answered. Much to my surprise, she seemed overjoyed to see me. I didn't know why; maybe it was because I gave her a nice card or because I'd been socializing with her lately. When she gave me a great big hug, I almost collapsed with happiness.

The whole thing with Savannah and Ms. Robertson's hating me was over. I'd done it! Victory was mine! She loved me now! I was on a major high for the rest of the day. I felt like I'd achieved something huge. Like I'd been failing academically but had suddenly gotten my grades up to all As.

*   *   *

My childhood friend, Ellen, was turning sixteen and would be having a sweet sixteen party. My parents, my sister, and I all went and had a great time at the party. However, my mind spent most of that night thinking about how the popular girls in school were starting to seriously torture me—and it was getting really bad.

On the way home from the party that night, my parents sat up front while I stared out the back window. Feeling miserable, I thought about the mistreatment I was receiving in school. I was scared and depressed.

I called Ellen on the phone as soon as I got home and told her what was going on in school. I felt so hopeless and powerless over the situation.

"Did this ever happen to you?" I asked Ellen. It had to have happened to someone else besides me!

"No," she said quietly.

I immediately felt alone and inferior. Something was definitely wrong with me. I was doing something wrong, I told myself. I had to be super weird to have all this bad stuff happen to me.

So, this is what I lived with. I was scared and anxious and full of dread. It didn't matter if I was simply opening the front door to leave the house, or walking down the streets in my neighborhood, visiting the library, standing in line in stores, waiting for the bus, or going to the park—I was constantly terrified.

Chapter 11

One afternoon in the cafeteria, I was busy showing all my New Kids buttons and pins to my friends when I realized that a couple of my buttons were missing. A group of popular girls were sitting right nearby, laughing. I knew they had my buttons.

I loved the New Kids, and I loved my buttons, so I went right up to their table and asked for my buttons back. They handed one back, but one of my favorites—a large one of Joe—was cracked. My heart sank. I loved that button. I was hurt that they'd do that, but I went back to my table to join my friends.

"Mary!" a voice shouted from behind me.

I looked back and one of the little bitches in the group was calling me.

"Come here," she said.

I felt stupid to have to get up and go over there again. But I felt I had no choice. As I walked over to them, they said a few ridiculous things to me that I blocked out. Seeing they'd called me over for no reason, I went back to my table.

"Mary!"

I ignored them. "Mary!" I still ignored them.

"Mary! Come here!" But I refused to humiliate myself by walking over to them like a lost dog.

Instead, Britney Anderson marched over to our table. The friends of mine who were sitting with me were Bella, Caitlin, and

Jan. Britney loomed over the four of us in our seats. My friends remained quiet as she taunted me and hurled insults at me.

Britney Anderson had apparently found out I'd said I was going to kick her ass, even though I didn't remember saying anything of the sort. Admittedly, I wouldn't have been surprised if I'd vented to a friend and those words had come out. Maybe someone overheard. Still, this came as a shock. When the hell did I say I'd kick her ass? And why would they ever think I'd even have the balls to say something like that?

Fake crying, Britney sarcastically said, "Oh, please don't kick my ass, Mary Powell, please don't kick my ass!"

I remembered what Bella's cousin had said at a party about standing up for myself. So I looked up at Britney and shot something at her. I told her to be quiet and a few other things. I added that she was always bothering people.

"What do you mean I'm always bothering people?" Britney said. She turned to my friends. "Caitlin, do I bother you?"

Caitlin shook her head as though what I'd said was completely wrong. "No!" she said emphatically.

"Jan, do I bother you?"

Jan shook her head and responded in the same tone, "No!"

Britney turned and looked down at Bella. "Bella, do I bother you?"

Bella didn't look at Britney. She was silent for a split second, then in an angry and quiet tone, she said, "No." I could tell she wasn't happy betraying me.

I was so hurt. I felt most betrayed by Caitlin. The way she said "no" seemed to come so quickly and naturally. She was supposed to be one of my best friends. I wanted to tell her I was angry with her, but I couldn't. Instead, when I got to science class that afternoon, I turned to Caitlin in the row next to mine.

As she sat, I stood. "Caitlin, I want you to know I totally understand why you had to say what you said to Britney today. And I want you to know that it won't bother me if you have to do it again."

She looked at me suspiciously and said, "Okay...okay." I think she knew I was bullshitting and that I felt exactly the opposite.

I added, "I won't ask you to stand up for me or anything like that." I couldn't say what I really wanted to say. I was basically telling Caitlin I *didn't* understand why she'd said that to Britney, that it *would* bother me if she had to do it again, and I *was* asking her to stand up for me—but using all the opposite words.

There was another time Britney Anderson stood by our table and verbally tortured me while my friends quietly sat by and watched. Britney's hand, mid-rant, happened to accidentally brush my hair.

When she realized what she'd done, she started screaming, "Eew! Eeeeew!"

She yelled this on purpose, for me and everyone else to see and hear. It was a big thing around school that my hair was gross and hated by all.

*   *   *

I was really coming to admire Ms. Robertson, although I couldn't put a finger on why.

One morning, I got to science class early. Ms. Robertson was just ending her homeroom class as I entered the room. I said hi to her and socialized with her briefly as I always did. Joking, I called Savannah a nerd. Ms. Robertson glared at me and told me not to call Savannah a nerd.

As she walked out of the classroom, Ms. Robertson stopped and looked at me. "If anyone's a nerd, Mary, it's you!" She walked away without another word.

I felt so stupid and embarrassed. I thought I deserved it, though. Even if I was only kidding, I shouldn't have called Savannah a nerd. I'd made myself look foolish and I'd put myself in that position. Of course, Ms. Robertson was right! Who was I to be calling anyone a nerd? I was a total dork, after all.

Another time, I got to science early and Ms. Robertson was speaking to another student. I made a negative joke about Howard Beach. The student with her turned around, glared at me, and told me not to talk that way about Howard Beach. Then Ms. Robertson, also annoyed, repeated exactly what the student had just said. I'd put my foot in my mouth again.

Still, I was becoming more and more attached to her. I found out that she was tutoring science after school on Mondays. Even though I wasn't having a ton of trouble in science, I wanted to make sure I did well this year to make up for my doing terribly the year before. So I sought out her help after school on Mondays.

I looked forward to both the tutoring and getting higher grades. I was already doing much better in science than I had in science last year, and that was very exciting for me. I was proud. I wanted Ms. Robertson to be involved with all this, so my father picked me up from tutoring every Monday night.

One such Monday, Ms. Robertson was sitting next to me. A student in my year was sitting on the other side of Ms. Robertson and venting about something to her. I wasn't listening. I was busy with doing my science work and I had a feeling that the student had a strong connection to Ms. Robertson. As I worked on a couple of problems, suddenly, Ms. Robertson said, "It's these *niggers*! They did it in Bensonhurst, and now they're doing it in Howard Beach."

I couldn't believe my ears. Did I hear her correctly? How could Ms. Robertson say that? Now I had to get used to the fact that Ms.

Robertson also had a bad side to her. But I decided to push it to the back of my mind. I adored her too much.

Ms. Robertson excused herself for a moment and left the table to do something. The student stood there, shaking her head. "Fucking niggers, I can't take them anymore," she muttered to me. Unsure of what to say, I stared at her in silence.

When Ms. Robertson came back and sat with me, she informed me she'd heard some of the girls in school were giving me a hard time.

She continued, "But I'm hearing some things, Mary. I understand you're giving people snotty looks?"

What? I thought. No way! I wasn't giving anyone snotty looks to cause the abuse I was getting. If anything, I went out of my way to avoid eye contact with those girls. To hear accusations of me doing otherwise was the opposite idea of myself. I wasn't someone who even stood up for herself, much less start with anyone. Regardless, it seemed as though Ms. Robertson was implying I was giving "looks" and that I was to blame for the teasing. I tried to protest, but it was futile.

On the phone that evening, Caitlin and I were in a discussion about Britney Anderson. Caitlin said, "Jan said, 'If Britney Anderson ever bothered me, I'd just take it!'" Caitlin then implied that she would do the same. This was apparently directed at me. Caitlin was giving me an indirect message to "just take it" whenever Britney bothered me.

Man, so had I made a mistake by opening my mouth to Britney instead of "just taking It"? Maybe if I had "just taken it," I would not be getting it so badly from Britney. Maybe she'd be around less.

Not only was Caitlin implying I wasn't doing things right, she told me that Jan thought so too. I was fucking up.

Britney Anderson continued to pick on me here and there.

In comparison to all the other popular girls, Britney appeared especially angry, bitter, and cruel. She often hung out with a girl named Tanya. Tanya was known to some of the ethnic minority students as the "traitor" black girl since she hung out with all the popular white girls. Britney had another very close friend named Jackie. I'd only ever seen Jackie from a distance because she wasn't in any of my classes, but it was obvious Jen was as tall and giraffe-like as Britney.

While I was sitting in the middle of the cafeteria, Tanya, the black traitor, came to our table and stood right by my chair while I ate. She looked down at me and said something about me having trouble with Britney Anderson. I indicated Britney was being cruel to me.

Tanya said provocatively, "So why don't you fight her?"

"No, thanks," I replied.

"Why? Do you think it's better to work things out peacefully? It's better to be nice and just talk things out?" She was mocking me, assuming that's what I was thinking. To be fair to her, she was right.

I didn't want to seem like a dork with sweet, corny beliefs, so I didn't answer honestly. Instead, I shook my head with disgust. "I'm not going to fight *her*." Meaning, Britney was beneath me and a waste of my time.

"Oooo!" Tanya shouted with delight as though she'd been given a million dollars. She ran off to deliver the message, laughing. No doubt she would tell Britney what I'd said, and they'd have a laugh over it before returning to bother me with it. I thought I was in huge trouble. But, to my relief, they never did come back.

*   *   *

Some of the other girls in my year had stopped bothering me

and so I started being a little more friendly with them. I believed it was all because the very popular Isabella was associating with me. One time when I was in the bathroom with Savannah, a popular girl named Kitty came in and started picking on her. Savannah asked Kitty if she was talking to me or to her. Kitty responded, "Mary?" She glanced at me with a confused face and said, "No, not Mary." For once, I was not the intended target.

Not long after this, however, I was in gym, standing alone on the gym floor with the class all around me. Some of the girls in the class were standing in their assigned places while others were moving around and playing a game. I don't know why, but I started feeling extremely uncomfortable being around the popular girls. I had to get away. I must have appeared upset because Kitty called out several times, "Mary! What's the matter?"

By this time, Kitty had accepted me, but now I was acting upset and distancing myself. I felt too shy and intimidated by Kitty and the other popular girls to simply revert to being friendly with them. I didn't respond to Kitty and turned away.

Even though Kitty had tried to reach out to me, I thought, yes, I appear okay on the outside, but really, I'm not. Really, I'm shy and withdrawn around popular kids, and nothing I did would ever change it. I just allowed my self-identity of being a dork to take over. It felt like something I couldn't control, something paralyzing me.

After that, Kitty started ignoring me. Instead, she joined in with others who picked on me, which had started up again since my episode in the gym.

From then on, everything started to become much, much worse.

More and more girls were bullying me, and the harsh treatment was becoming more frequent and more intense. They were mainly in the form of personal insults and laughing—usually by several girls at a time. It was hard to avoid their taunts.

My victimization could happen anywhere, in any and all of my classes, gym being the worst since it was unstructured. At lunch, outside, inside, in the hallway, by the lockers. Sometimes I felt safe, such as when I was with my friends. The bullying happened the least when I was with my friends or when I was in class during lectures. The rest of the time, I was considered fair game.

One time, I had been assigned to sit on the floor in gym near the bleachers. Britney Anderson and Isabella sat nearby. I heard Britney say, "Mary Powell." She then turned to Isabella and said something about me. Isabella replied with something negative about me, making sure it was loud enough for me to hear.

I felt hurt and betrayed. I had thought Isabella liked me! This was a huge shock to me because there was no warning from her; it just came out of nowhere. In fact, we'd had a perfectly pleasant conversation only the day before.

There were a few times after this when Isabella was nice to me again. I didn't know what to make of her chalk and cheese attitude toward me. I just figured she had mixed feelings about our friendship.

In passing, I told Isabella that Savannah had said something negative about her. Talking horribly about Savannah was basically the only thing that held Isabella and me together.

Shortly after, I was sitting with my friends in homeroom when Isabella shouted across the room, "Mary! Come here."

Although I felt very intimidated and scared—I *never* went to that side of the room—of course I was going to obey. I walked over to Isabella's desk and she told me to confirm that Savannah had said something bad about her. Again, I obeyed.

Isabella's best friend Nicoletta—whom I hated and knew hated me—slowly lifted up her head from the desk.

"What did Savannah say?" she demanded.

I repeated again what Savannah had said.

She glared at me and spat, "Does she want a slap in the face?"

Was she talking to me, too?

Isabella, in a friendly way, instructed me to take the bus home that afternoon with Savannah and to make sure we stood near her and her friends on the bus.

That afternoon, as directed, Savannah and I took the bus home and we stood near Isabella and her friends. By now, word of Isabella's plan had spread to a whole group of their friends, at least eight of them.

Emma—"Dizzy" from science—was one of the girls who sat with Isabella and Nicoletta. I was standing next to Savannah, who was now seated behind this group of girls.

Emma looked up at me. "Mary!" she said, gesturing to me to lean down to her. She asked as a whisper in my ear what it was that Savannah had said about Isabella. I whispered the answer and stood back up.

Emma then turned around in her seat and confronted Savannah out loud. Savannah denied it over and over as Emma continued to probe her.

Emma turned back around and looked up at me. "Mary."

I was scared that Emma would beckon to me like that, especially right in front of Savannah, making it obvious what I'd done. I had my suspicions that Emma had done it on purpose.

As I leaned down again, she said, "I thought you said Savannah said..." and she repeated what she understood was the story.

Emma had misinterpreted my words. So I said, "No, you misunderstood me." I regretted those words as soon as I said them.

Emma protested in a loud voice and then laughed at me, as did the other girls, including Isabella.

Feeling humiliated and betrayed by Isabella, I couldn't help but wonder why she would just go against me like that. From Savannah to me and back again. From one to the other. I thought I was on their side! But no, they'd strung me along.

After the scene on the bus, the teasing of me increased even further, while it seemed to be happening less and less to Savannah. Isabella no longer spoke to me. Britney Anderson, whom I grew increasingly terrified of, continued to torment me at every opportunity, literally whenever she saw me.

*   *   *

A few days later, I was confronted by a couple of classmates with a rumor that I'd called Isabella "an asshole." I was totally shocked at that. Who the hell had made this one up? Then again, I had been so upset and angry at Isabella that I could have easily vented to someone, and who knows what had come out of my mouth. Either way, I honestly didn't remember calling Isabella an asshole. So I outright denied it.

I went into the bathroom with Bella during lunch only to find Emma and her friend standing by the mirrors.

Emma asked calmly, "Mary, what happened with you and Isabella?"

Glad to have an opportunity to clear my name, I explained in an upset tone, "She thinks I called her an asshole. I didn't say that. I don't know why everyone's saying that. I don't think she's an asshole."

Conscious of Bella's presence behind me, I thought, she knows I'm selling myself out. I wished she wasn't there.

Emma and her friend said nothing in reply to my plea, so Bella and I left the bathroom and went back to our table in the cafeteria. A group of girls, including Isabella and Angelica, approached our table. They confronted me and accused me of calling Isabella an asshole.

Isabella glared at me. "Why did you say that, Mary? I was nice to you!" It was as though she had done me a favor. Why should she bother to be nice to someone like me?

Fear caused me to play the role. "I know," I said, hoping she wouldn't be mad.

She scowled at me and bent down within inches of my face. "You're going to get jumped," she growled. "You *and* your friend."

I tried to plead with her as she walked away, but Angelica the god looked at me threateningly and said, "What? Did you say..." Angelica thought I'd said something negative, but I explained she'd misheard me, and she walked away in a huff.

Things, of course, got worse and worse. Britney Anderson tormented me severely and Tanya—the black "traitor"—assisted Britney in her efforts, as did a couple of others. To me, Britney had the scariest face, look, and voice out of all of them.

*　　*　　*

One night several weeks earlier, Bella had had a party at her house. She often had great parties and I always had a lot of fun at them. At one point during the party, Bella and I were hanging out in the doorway with one of Bella's cousins. We had gotten to talking about Britney Anderson and what was going on for me in school.

Bella's cousin had insisted that I fight back, regardless of the fact that it would pretty much be me against a bunch of them. She asked me what Britney looked like. I told her she reminded me of a certain goofy TV star. She doubled over laughing and insisted even more persistently that I must fight back.

My bullies had never gotten physical with me. Physical fights happened at our school very rarely. So, fighting back in this case would mean a verbal attack. I asked Bella's cousin about the consequences. What if it caused more problems? What if it made them become even more angry?

She told me none of that mattered and it would all be fine "as long as I settled the score." A part of me thought she was right, but another part of me knew retaliating would be dangerous. The more I thought about doing it, the more terrified I felt. But the way she made my situation sound also made me feel a fresh wave of anger toward these girls. It did make me want to lash out at them.

On Monday, when Britney Anderson and her friends tortured me, I stood up for myself, albeit in quite a timid fashion. I instantly regretted it. My attempted defense only got them even more riled up and caused them to torture me even more.

In gym one morning, it felt like the entire world around me either hated me or thought I was a disgusting joke. It was a horrible feeling. As I stood in my spot on the gym floor, I heard comments being yelled at me from all directions.

Our gym class had to do this square-dancing thing, but whichever girls I had to dance with always looked away in disgust and squealed whenever they touched me. I felt terrible.

One of these girls was Ann, a girl I'd talked to once or twice. She was apparently highly amused that she was dancing with me. She threw her head back in laughter and other people were laughing along with her. I was so hurt. They were yelling, "Go, Ann!" It was a nightmare. My entire being was consumed with vulnerability and fear.

Next, I had to dance with Angelica—the "god." She had a miserable face, all stone-like because she had to dance with me. We weren't arm in arm like we were supposed to be; she simply placed the very tip of her finger on my wrist. Her face looked as though she'd just been given a death sentence.

She hated me. She thought I was gross. It was as though her feelings toward me were being transferred through our contact, however minimal. I felt sick. I felt a sense of doom. Like someone I loved had just passed away. Like I was being abused.

When gym class was over, I hurried back to the locker room. Tanya yelled my name and announced, "She has white hair just like my grandma!"

Ouch. She had gotten me on one of my most sensitive areas. I had, since I was eleven, some premature grays. Being hereditary, I'd gotten this problem from my mother, but no one had ever made a joke about it before. Now though, someone had finally hit me where it really hurt. My gray hair.

As I got to the door of the locker room, Kitty stood in front of me, backing up as I walked forward. She was laughing. She was apparently amused that I had danced with Angelica the god.

"Mary!" she shouted in my face, "Do you *love* Angelica? Do you want to kiss Angelica? Do you want to *marry* Angelica?"

Her questions were even more humiliating than the comments about my grandma-like hair. I had just as much teen homophobia as anyone. Her accusations were probably the worst thing someone could ever imply. She doubled over in hysterics, right in front of the door I was trying to escape through.

I had to get through that door, and there was no way I was going to let her and her stupid antics stop me. Her being physical was when I decided it had gone too far. Even I wouldn't put up with that, regardless of what they might do to me.

I lightly shoved her out of the way and opened the door. She looked confused and said, "Ow!" It seemed like she hadn't realized I'd pushed her. Whether she had or not, she never did anything about it. Thankfully, nor did anyone else. I was proud of myself because, at that very moment when I'd shoved her out of the way, I didn't feel afraid—at least, I hadn't for that split second. I felt strangely confident about my physical fighting ability.

After gym, Bella walked with me quietly to lunch. I felt like I was going to start crying. I rarely cried in front of people. In fact, I couldn't remember the last time I'd cried in school. You just didn't do that, especially after being bullied. I tried desperately hard to hold back the tears.

But I knew Bella saw. When we got to the front of the cafeteria, the tears stung my eyes and my chest started heaving.

Bella said gently, "Your eyes are watering. Maybe you should go wash your face."

"Yeah, I'm going to the bathroom," I responded before hurrying away.

In the bathroom, I shut myself in one of the stalls and cried quietly. The pain in my chest was nothing compared to the pain in my heart.

When I went back to the cafeteria, a large group of girls teased me beyond belief. Whatever they said and did was so traumatic that I completely blocked everything out. Instead, I got the hell out of there and ran through the halls of the school building, unsure of where I was even heading.

I must have run a full circle because I somehow ended up back at the cafeteria. Debating whether or not to go back in, I was shaking from head to toe. Anyone could be in there by now, waiting for me.

As I peeked my head through the doorway, I saw Tanya in a group.

"There she is!" she shouted, pointing at me as though she were instructing people to go after me.

When I saw Tanya point and yell, everything hit me like I'd collided with a bus. I couldn't believe it. It was the worst moment

I ever had in school. No one had ever pointed me out directly and instructed people to come and get me. As bad as things had gotten for me socially, it had never come to that before.

But no one came out of the cafeteria to get me. I stayed out of the cafeteria for the rest of the day and vowed not to go to lunch there ever again.

Feeling like I needed protection, I called my father and asked him to pick me up. I was too scared to leave when everyone else was leaving and would be outside in the open.

When school ended for the day, I sat on the bleachers in the gym. I was alone. That was until Britney Anderson stuck her head in the door.

To my surprise, she was nice! "Mary, were you crying? Was it because of what I did?"

I didn't want to let her know she'd gotten to me, that she'd made me cry. You didn't do stupid things like that. So I made up an excuse for why I'd been crying.

"Oh, okay. I was just making sure it wasn't because of me," she said. Then she smiled and started a friendly conversation. I was amazed she was actually talking to me, even if it was only for a minute.

As doom descended all around me, I told myself that was the worst day I'd ever had in school, and possibly the worst day of my entire life. I was so depressed and in despair that I once again thought I might have to transfer schools.

Chapter 12

During lunch one day in the cafeteria while I was sitting with some of my friends, a senior came to me and introduced herself. She said her name was Amanda. She was nice with me, almost professional, and she said that she'd heard Britney Anderson was bothering me. As it turned out, she'd also had major problems with Britney, and she explained that, if I wanted to, we could join together and get Britney in trouble. It was suggested we could report something to the principal, Sr. Agatha. I wholeheartedly agreed with her idea.

With nowhere else to go after lunch, I went to religion class early and sat in my seat. An acquaintance of Savannah came into the classroom, even though she wasn't in the class, and sat a couple of desks in front of me. She wasn't one of the really popular girls, but she lived near Savannah and I said hi to her sometimes. I'd always thought she was okay.

"Mary," she said, "I hear you're starting with Britney Anderson?"

I looked away from her and shook my head. "No, I'm not starting with Britney...Britney's starting with me."

"Okay, okay," she said. "Just...look. The thing is, if you do start with Britney, then..." She paused. "I'm going to have to get involved."

I felt betrayed. I thought this girl was okay, especially because she was friendly to Savannah. What was this? Who was next?

I again insisted I wasn't bothering Britney. With other people now entering the room and watching, she pushed a chair back and walked out, saying, "Okay. Just...just stay away from her."

When I told Bella about the threats, she said she thought this girl was a joke and simply mocked her.

I decided to keep the vow I'd made about not attending lunch period. I didn't want to go anymore.

After a couple of days, I finally went to the principal, Sr. Agatha, to talk to her about everything that had been going on. She needed to know.

Sr. Agatha was a tall nun. She was somewhat intimidating to me, but I think that was more because she was the principal than anything else. Her office was all the way down at the end of the long hallway on the first floor, at the opposite end of where the cafeteria was. The location was kind of deserted and quiet. It felt isolated. The empty waiting room had the desk where the nun who'd since passed used to work. No one else was around, so I gently knocked on Sr. Agatha's office door and she called me in.

I sat down and started to tell her what was going on. At first, I felt like she was being unsupportive. It seemed as though there wasn't much she could do. Angry at her for her lack of understanding, I involuntarily began to cry. Sr. Agatha stood up, became quiet, and handed me a box of tissues. She took a tissue herself and held it to her nose. Then, she walked back and forth without saying a word.

I hadn't wanted to meet with her in the first place, so I felt even more embarrassed about crying. Why was I alone with her? And why had it come down to this? Not only was I sitting in the principal's office, I was telling on people too!

I crumbled the tissue in my palm. "I mean...maybe they don't know what they're doing. Maybe they don't know it bothers me, maybe they don't know it hurts."

"Oh, yeah. They know, they know," she said, still walking back and forth.

How could that be? They knew? These girls knew how much they could hurt someone yet they did it anyway?

Amanda, the girl who had told me she wanted to do something about Britney Anderson, had a plan.

So, in a classroom on the first floor several days later, Sr. Agatha sat at the teacher's desk and Amanda and I sat in the front row, along with Britney Anderson, Kitty, Tanya, and a few others from the main group of girls who were the guiltiest.

Amanda spoke most of the time. Sr. Agatha then asked Britney what was going on with her and Amanda. Britney looked down and said, "Well...Amanda and I don't really get along too well." There was something like a personal history between the two of them.

Then it was my turn. Sr. Agatha confronted the group on how they'd been treating me. They were quiet, like they'd been busted. There wasn't much they could do. This was the principal after all, and they knew she was on my side.

I mentioned an incident where Kitty had been nasty to me. Kitty responded that she was only trying to return my vocabulary book.

But I described to Sr. Agatha how it happened. I had been sitting on the floor of the gym when Kitty walked over and looked down at me. "Is this your book?" she'd asked. I recognized it in her hand and said it was. She'd then slammed it down on the floor in front of me and said, "Here, take it! You left it on my fucking desk!"

Sr. Agatha looked at Kitty. "That's how you returned her book? That's what you're talking about, Kitty?"

Kitty looked embarrassed. "Well..."

One of the other girls happened to mention lunch period, but Sr. Agatha interrupted her. "Do you mean the lunch period that Mary doesn't even go to anymore? Is that the one you're talking about? Mary isn't even going to lunch because of what you people are doing to her."

Now it was my turn to be embarrassed. I didn't want the girls to know how badly they'd gotten to me. That would only show I was scared.

At one point, Sr. Agatha got very angry at Britney Anderson and criticized her. Britney was looking down.

"'Cause you're a dime a dozen, babe!" she scolded. I wasn't really sure what Sr. Agatha meant, but whatever it meant, I knew it was an insult.

I told one of my friends about it later, and she started laughing and clapping. "Good! Good!" she said.

The teasing and torturing cooled down after the meeting. Not completely, but somewhat.

*   *   *

Unbelievably, other than the bullying, sophomore year ended up being an absolute blast for me. I was making so many friends, and I was learning how to separate the bad from the good. I didn't let those horrible girls stop me from having fun with my friends. My friends still accepted me, although not all the time. Sometimes, I got to be too much with my hyperactivity and they could be harshly critical. Yet they still loved me. It was weird.

I had joined the aerobics team as well as dance that year in Blue and Gold. I was so into the annual competition and really looking forward to it. As a sophomore, this year I was on the gold team. Danielle, the school's "queen of dancing," had been the freshman assistant captain the year before but was now the captain of dance. I rolled my eyes at the thought; she was indeed a "queen," and all the students thought she was so wonderful.

The theme this year was called "A Girl for All Seasons," so the routines all had to have something to do with the seasons of the year, the weather or whatever. Our dance team was dancing to "It's Raining Men." My aerobics team was using the song, "Walking on Sunshine." I did struggle with the routines somewhat, but over the course of the practices, I did get them down pat.

I felt I did terribly with dance on the first night of Blue and Gold, so much so that people were teasing me. I went to the bleachers where Savannah and Bella were and cried. They tried to support me and encourage me, but I was already too upset and humiliated by that point.

The next night, however, I did great. I also looked much better, which kind of made up for the night before.

Our dance team won, but our aerobics team lost. Gold won the Blue and Gold overall. To know that we'd won a second year in a row made me really excited. To be fair, the people in my year were really good dancers, so I was quite confident we were going to win every year.

*　　*　　*

I was having more and more fun and I laughed hysterically every day. School had become a place where all my friends were. Acting wild and having a lot of friends were the reasons I became happy. I'd never been in that position before.

My friends meant everything to me, and I would do anything to prove that to them. I'd also do anything to get them to like me even more. One day, Caitlin told me she was having problems with her friend, Sandra, who was apparently no longer acting like a friend and being kind of mean to her instead.

I told Caitlin I'd take the bus with her to Howard Beach, which was where they all lived, and "take care of it." I knew of this girl

Sandra, and she wasn't anything to be afraid of; she wasn't a threat. Nor was she popular. But she was bothering Caitlin, and I loved Caitlin. I'd become very loyal to my friends and would get angry at the thought of them being mistreated.

In the little culture I was living in, if someone bothers your friend, you take care of them. That's what most of the girls at Stella did, so that's what I'd do—even though none of my friends were doing that for me. Thanks to observing how the popular girls bothered and made fun of people, including me, I had a good idea of how to do it myself.

So, one afternoon after school, I took the bus with Caitlin and a couple of her friends. As the bus dropped more people off and became less crowded, I went up to the front of the bus, which was where Sandra was sitting. I made sure it was obvious to Sandra that I was with Caitlin and that I was on Caitlin's side.

I dropped myself down next to Sandra, banging into her as I sat down. "Whoops! I'm sorry," I said. I noticed Caitlin and a couple of others start to laugh.

Then I "accidentally" threw the wrapper of the candy bar I'd been eating at Sandra. "Oh, I'm sorry!" I said again.

I said and did a couple of other things, then I got off the bus with Caitlin. She was really grateful for what I'd done. After that, she seemed to really like me and we became closer. One evening after I'd been studying at Caitlin's, her father drove me home. I sat in the back and Caitlin was in the passenger seat.

"Mary, I want to thank you for what you did for my daughter," he said.

Wow. I didn't think I'd done much at all. All I'd done was bang into a girl a couple of times and throw a candy wrapper.

The next day at lunch, Caitlin laughed and told me that Sandra had gotten really angry and said to her something like, "And I don't appreciate how you got *Mary Powell* to do that to me. *Mary Powell* shouldn't have..."

I hated how Sandra used my first and last name. It reminded me of how the popular girls called me the same. Did that mean she saw me as a nothing, too? Did she also see me as a loser and that the only reason she let me win was because she was all by herself?

Jan, at lunch, told me that Savannah had laughed and said, "Just watch Mary get involved."

Jan said to me, "Savannah knows you so well!"

Even though she'd said it with humor, it bothered me. I didn't want Savannah to "know me" and be right about me. I didn't like being close with Savannah. Yuck, she was such a loser!

*　　*　　*

I had become close friends with a girl named Mellie and her best friend Liz. The more friends I had, the happier I was and the "cooler" I felt. I was happy to be friends with Liz because she was pretty and looked like the popular type, even though she wasn't. People dismissed her or ignored her. Supposedly, she was a fake.

Once, Liz borrowed my vocabulary book required for English. When I needed it back, it turned out she'd lost it. So, in class, when we were asked to use it, I announced I didn't have my book and explained why.

To get a new vocabulary book from our English teacher was ten dollars. I didn't have ten dollars, so I said I would try to get the book back from Liz.

Liz still didn't provide the book and was vague about its whereabouts. It quickly became a full-on discussion in front of the whole class, all about my book.

One girl shouted to me from across the room, "You shouldn't

have lent her your book."

It sounded to me like this was said in a blame-the-victim way, but I couldn't afford to respond negatively so I quickly came up with an answer.

"Well, I know that now." This way, I was validating the statement from the girl, but placing blame on Liz, not me, and I was also publicly insulting someone unpopular, which made me look good.

Another girl, who sat in front of me, shook her head disgustedly and went up to the teacher's desk. "This is for Mary's book," she said, placing ten dollars in front of the teacher. "Liz Masters...um... she can't handle this."

The class started cheering. I guess people didn't really like Liz. I was also flattered that this girl would do that for me. Again, it made me look good that another student was supporting me, one who wasn't unpopular. I was shocked the class had clapped in a positive way regarding something that was in any way related to me.

I was also chatting with other girls who were well-liked. One such popular girl sat next to me in homeroom, but she was really nice. She'd been the one who said if young Alex treated me right, age didn't matter. As a bonus, she couldn't stand Britney Anderson either. Her mother and my mother chatted a little once at an open house meeting. Unfortunately for me, she transferred to another school in the middle of that year.

After she'd left, Minnie ended up sitting next to me instead. She was an old friend of Cathy's, and very eccentric. She was really crazy and funny. While she wasn't popular, she wasn't unpopular either. Caitlin, who also held the same "not popular but not unpopular" status, sat behind Minnie.

Behind me was a girl who had transferred to Stella in sophomore year. She was really cool. While she became friends with the popular girls, in homeroom, she always stayed at our corner and never left us. Plus, she never made fun of me.

In front of me was Annie. She was a friend of Britney Anderson's and a friend of Britney's best friend. However, Annie was nothing like them. She was never mean, she was always very nice, and I enjoyed talking to her. Half the time, she would be asleep on her desk. She was kind of a Barbie Doll type.

Annie told me she couldn't stand Ms. Robertson. "One time, in class, she said my textbook was 'worn and torn.' So I said, 'Yeah, so are you.' Then she yelled at me, 'Get out! Get out of my classroom!' And she threw me out." Unable to process the rest of her story, I was too busy thinking about what Annie meant when she said Ms. Robertson was "worn and torn." It felt disgusting somehow.

*　　*　　*

The weather was getting warmer and the end of my sophomore year was drawing closer. My former junior high school was having its annual bazaar, and on one of the nights of the bazaar, I saw a guy there who was often at the bus stop to go to school. I knew he went to the public high school by Stella because he would get off there every morning.

I had taken several glances at him before. I thought he might be cute when I'd seen him from a distance, but then I'd seen more closely and realized he wasn't as cute as I'd thought. So I'd never done anything about it. Because I got used to seeing him every morning, I ended up just seeing him as some kind of dork.

When I saw him at the bazaar, though, we wound up talking. You know what, I thought, he is kind of cute. Maybe I will pursue this. His name was Craig, and I hung out with him and a few of his friends that night.

At one point, one of his friends said, "It's ten-thirty, and if I don't get laid—" Craig started laughing and stopped him from finishing his sentence by punching his arm. I felt uncomfortable.

Later on that night, Craig and I went off alone to the church steps where we talked for what felt like hours. We were still talking as the bazaar closed up and everyone started to go home. It had to be about midnight.

I was feeling shy and kind of intimidated by this guy. He was talking up a storm, although I did notice he had quite a negative attitude and could be a bit too condescending for my liking.

After talking for a while longer, he shuffled up right next to me so that his body was touching mine. A part of me wanted to kiss him, but I believed in the guy making the first move.

He finally leaned over to kiss me, but then he did a weird thing and put his tongue in my mouth. I had heard of people doing this when they kissed. Apparently, it was called a "French kiss." The way it sounded, I thought it was just a special, rare form of kissing. Now he was doing it to me.

I was totally grossed out. This was disgusting. I had thought, having watched tons of movies and TV, that people kissed just using their lips.

Nevertheless, I let him do it, and then I did it back. I figured I had to go along with it. If a guy does something physical to you, you take it.

Craig then laid me down on the steps and lay on top of me as we continued tongue-kissing. No one else was around by this time. It was late, it was very dark, and we were alone.

Peeking over his shoulder, I noticed my father crossing over to our side of the street.

"Oh, shit, it's my father." Craig quickly pulled himself off me and sat next to me with an innocent smile on his face.

My father had seen what we were doing. He said hi and

continued to walk toward home. I knew he had to be bothered about what he'd just seen.

With my father out of sight, we continued kissing for a while, but I eventually said I had to get home. Craig walked me as far as the corner where my house was; I didn't want us to go any nearer, not together.

Standing lightly pressed up against a guy was the way I'd imagined kissing. It was so weird and so exciting to finally have really kissed someone. But the thing was, I didn't feel a lot of attraction. As he kissed me good night, he squeezed my rear end. The unexpected move made me feel slightly uncomfortable. I didn't even get why he did it.

At home, my mother said my father had told her a guy was lying on top of me and that we were kissing. She also said I wasn't in trouble.

So, I had a boyfriend now, and we talked on the phone here and there to begin with.

We made a date to go to the movies. This would be my first ever official date. There was a part of me that really didn't want to be with this guy. I was kind of repulsed by him. But he wanted to date me, and he was kind of cute, so I felt I had to.

I was at Savannah's house the day of the date, and I told her all about my ambivalent feelings. Craig said he would be coming to Savannah's house in a cab to pick me up.

When I got in the cab with him, a big part of me felt I was doing the wrong thing. It was the first time I'd ever chosen a guy over my friends, and I thought about how I could have rescheduled the date for a day I wasn't with Savannah. Because I was leaving Savannah in the late afternoon and not later at night like I normally did, it felt as though this date was cutting into my time with my friend. Thanks to my unreasonable addiction to fantasies of romance, relationships, and guys, I felt I had to go through with it. I wasn't in control.

Craig was sitting on one side of the cab by the window in the backseat, and I sat all the way on the other end. After a while, he leaned over and started kissing me.

It was awkward for me, us kissing while the driver was sitting there right in front of us. This cab driver thinks we're boyfriend and girlfriend. It's public.

By the time we'd seen the movie, which I thought sucked, I'd decided I was not attracted to Craig and wanted to go home.

During the cab ride home, I had a feeling that our time together had not been a good date. I definitely knew that I hadn't had a good time, and that for my first date in my entire life, it was absolutely awful. I didn't really like him anyway. He seemed like a jerk that primarily cared about the physical stuff, not to mention he had cut into my time with my friends.

Chapter 13

My father was becoming increasingly angry and having violent outbursts. He had no problem yelling at us and hitting us—mainly me—whenever he felt slighted. I tended to stand up for myself to my parents, so I got the worst treatment and most of the physical violence. A number of questions puzzled me back then. Why am I so social at home but not elsewhere? Why can I tell off my parents and siblings without a problem but not anyone outside the family?

I had my brothers thinking I was someone I wasn't. I had them thinking I was a tough girl. My mother told me James had said the girls in his school were "tough like Mary." I felt like a liar, a fraud, and ashamed of myself when I heard that. Because that wasn't me! I wasn't "tough" or cool. I was a dork and a disappointment to everyone—myself and my family.

Serving as a much needed relief from home, Bella, Jordan, India, Savannah, Jodi, and I went to the beach one day in May after school. Surprisingly, going to the beach was a rarity, even though it was right behind the school. It was exciting and joyful, not only because it symbolized summer was coming but also the end of the school year as well.

On the blanket in the sand, one of the girls decided to do my hair in a different style, which was a subtle way of saying no one liked the way I did my hair. She French-braided it, something I couldn't do with my own hair, though I could manage a half-decent effort with others.

As my hair was being done, the other girls all stared at the process and made compliments about how nice it looked. I felt uncomfortable, like I was under a microscope. I was being complimented but insulted at the same time. What they really meant was, "It looks better than your normal style, Mary."

Despite feeling like I was on display on that blanket, I loved how my hair came out with the French braid. I felt like I looked normal for once.

We all had such a great time at the beach. Jordan, India, and I chased each other by the water and dunked each other in. Of course, I got dunked the most. The way they did it didn't feel tormenting, rather that I was popular with them.

After our sunny afternoon on the beach, I went home on a real high. I went to the park later and thought about the wonderful time we'd all had as I walked about and sat on the swings. I daydreamed about it and replayed it over and over in my mind.

*   *   *

I took the history Regents. Although I was certain I was going to fail, I was determined to work my butt off on it and wrote the material my father had taught me in all the essays.

As the Regents exams were handed out, a student in the next row said jokingly, "Oh, Lordy, Lordy, Lordy." People started laughing.

I filled the essays with as much information as I could, bullshitting to the umpteenth degree on anything I didn't know. By the time I put down my pen, I was really scared I'd failed. It was a much harder test than I'd expected.

With the last day of Regents exams over, I got a call at home that evening from Caitlin.

"Did you get a call?" She was asking if a teacher had called to tell me I'd failed the Regents.

"No," I said.

"Mary, I think we're in the clear!"

I was in the living room by the piano when she said that. I'd passed? Wow. If Caitlin said I'm safe, then it must be okay.

I wound up passing history by the skin of my teeth. I got a sixty-five. Either I was just about good enough to pass it or that crazy nun was feeling generous and just passed me out of sympathy. Math and Spanish I also barely passed.

Science, I was disappointed with. I got an eighty-one. Even though, for me, that was a very high score on a Regents, I was hoping to get much higher. Especially since I'd done well in the class and had worked extra hard with my studying and additional tutoring with Ms. Robertson.

When I told Savannah my science score, she then told me she got an eighty-two. Her tone suggested she was lying and just trying to beat me. It was sad, but that's how our friendship was. We were friends, yet we often despised each other, even though it was mostly unspoken.

We'd have little spats here and there. Childish ones. Once, I made fun of her weight when we were walking up the stairs between classes. She wasn't overweight, she just wasn't skinny like I was.

"Shut up, Mary. You have Jew curls," she said. She meant my hair was naturally curly and was insulting the way it looked, which bothered me tremendously.

She was unbelievable. She was racist and made a habit of insulting certain people behind their back. She was always nice to their face. She insulted Jewish people yet seemed to really like my Jewish friend, Ellen. Once, Savannah and Ellen sat together on my living room couch. Savannah said, "Wow, I really like your bracelet."

Ellen replied, "Thank you! I really like your sweater!"

"Thank you! Your hair looks pretty!"

"Thank you!"

And so it went on.

"My God, you guys are so polite," I said.

Ellen burst out laughing as Savannah smirked and said, "Oh shut up, Mary."

Really, I was glad Savannah was so nice to Ellen. Maybe exposure to the actual person behind the stereotype was good for her. But I also thought she was a hypocrite.

Racism went on all over the place in my school. And not just by the white girls. By the Hispanic and the Puerto Rican girls hating the Dominican girls and vice versa. Not that I was innocent. I was totally against racism, but I also found myself, like everyone else, using racial slurs to describe people I didn't like. It was in the same way I used words such as "slut," "fat," and "bitch" to describe girls I didn't like. It was really about culture and my immediate environment that I identified with. The culture of the girls in school was to use those words and have those attitudes. Sometimes, I played along with it simply to fit in.

*　　*　　*

I was so happy and excited to be preparing for my sweet sixteen. I'd decided to have a theme—two, actually. They were: New Kids on the Block, and the colors black and white. I required everyone to wear a combination of black or white to the party and, if they were fans, to bring or wear something related to NKOTB, such as buttons or pins.

The DJ was the same one Bella had used for her parties. My

parents paid his fee of two hundred dollars, but they told me the DJ and the party would be my sweet sixteen gift. At least, that's what my father told me, claiming they couldn't afford to get me anything else.

My grandfather and his wife wound up sending me two hundred dollars in my birthday card, saying it was to pay for the DJ. I am pretty sure my father insisted my parents keep that money or at least take a portion of it. After all, he stated it was meant for the DJ, which was what they'd paid for. That was disappointing because I would have liked the money for myself.

A couple of days before my sweet sixteen, I started cleaning the back yard. It wasn't the nicest back yard, but I'd work on it and at least make it festive.

I spent hours sweeping all the dirt and heavy dust off the concrete and in the driveway. I picked up garbage, old toys, and deflated balls that were scattered around the lawn and under the huge blossom bush we had. To ensure a good first impression for my party guests, I used a pale yellow paint to go over the front of the chipped garage. I thought it looked pretty good.

When the paint was dry, I used construction paper to cut out large letters in black and white, which spelled out "Mary's Sweet 16" for the top line, "Black and White" for the middle, and "NKOTB" for the bottom.

I hung black and white crepe paper over the top of the garage and on the porch, and I pinned up black and white balloons all over. Everything looked great, and I'd done it all myself.

Almost everyone I'd invited turned up at the party, which started in the early evening when it was still sunny out. Savannah and Jetta gave me their gift in my house before running out to the backyard. When I opened the gift, I looked at the envelope and read out loud, "Mary Carol Elizabeth Powell." Jetta had written my whole name, including my confirmation name. I didn't know why. Now I realize they were making fun of me and my name. It felt weird.

Bella, who was busy walking back and forth in the back yard to make sure everything was set up for the DJ, made me feel a little better. I was flattered that she wanted to make sure everything was right for my party. It made me feel important and that I deserved effort from other people.

Filled with pride, I took a photo of my crowd of friends. Everyone was dressed in black and white, or one of the colors, and some of them held up buttons and pins of NKOTB.

Bella's DJ was amazing and had everyone up dancing and singing all night. I was dancing like crazy, being silly and making people laugh—probably *at* me, but whatever, I was used to it.

Later in the evening, we had my cake. I made a dramatic speech over how much I appreciated everyone being there before I blew out my candles. Most people, as normal, didn't exhibit the same enthusiasm. I assumed they just saw me as being "hyper Mary."

I'd said I didn't want my parents at the party; no adults at all for that matter. So they remained indoors with Ellen's parents in the living room.

As it got late, Minnie—Cathy's eccentric friend—came into the kitchen with her friend to talk to me. "Mary, where are the guys? You have no guys at your party?" She said it in a mocking way.

At this time, I was still dating Craig—at least in my head—even though I'd only seen him twice in the last three months. I told Minnie that my boyfriend and his friends were supposed to come but I didn't know where they were.

When they continued to mock the party because there were no guys, I stormed upstairs and called Craig. It sounded like he wasn't alone when I called, so I figured he and some of his friends were getting ready to come to the party. He said he would, but he never showed up.

Minnie and her friend continued to mock me about the "no guys" thing when I came back downstairs. As they left the kitchen, laughing and snickering, I sat at the table alone and started to cry.

Jodi came in from outside and saw me crying. Feeling embarrassed, I desperately wanted to stop, but I was so hurt. I felt a little stupid for being hurt by Craig, but Minnie and her friend were the ones that had really made me furious.

Jodi began to hug me when I told her what they said. Bella and her cousin also came inside and comforted me. They said it was Minnie and her friend's problem if they didn't like the party. I appreciated their support, but I still didn't feel a whole lot better. Why should I have felt better? I didn't have any guys at the party. My party is pathetic, I told myself. And I'm pathetic, as always. No matter how hard I tried, I couldn't get Minnie out of my head.

After sulking for a while longer, I went back outside to dance with my friends. I whispered to Jodi, "I'm not wearing a bra!"

Jodi gasped. "You're not wearing a bra? Why?" She acted like I'd done something freaky or terribly wrong.

"I thought it was going to show with this shirt," I explained, pointing to the strappy, cut-off black shirt I was wearing. The last thing I needed was my white bra sticking out.

Again, I felt like a freak, embarrassed by my big, bare breasts. I should have been wearing a bra. Now I felt naked, like breasts were something to be ashamed of, to be hidden away.

Earlier that day, I'd made a large sign out of oak tag to allow people to write birthday messages to me. I noticed everyone had written on it, and some of the notes were really sweet. Then, there was Jodi's, which she had written earlier, before she found me crying. It said, "Did your mother ever have any children that lived?" I had no idea what it meant. I knew Jodi would get annoyed at me at times for being so hyper. But what did her message mean? Was she saying I was brain dead or something?

Later, Caitlin said with a disgusted look as though she didn't like Laura, "Did you see what Jodi wrote? What a bitch!"

I only half-agreed with Caitlin, even though I knew she was right. But I couldn't always see when I was being disrespected. I didn't get that I deserved to be angry with the way some people treated me.

At the end of the night, Bella stomped in the house shouting, "Your stupid neighbors said it's time to shut the music off. It's only eleven o'clock! They agreed that you'd be having a party, right? And they knew you'd have a DJ. What the fuck is that all about?"

I was disappointed, too, but my neighbors, the ones that shared our back yard, told my parents they wanted the DJ off, so the DJ went off. Bella and her family wanted to tell my neighbors what they really thought of them, but I begged for them not to.

Anyway, that was my sweet sixteen. For a while, because of Minnie, I felt bad about the way my party had gone down, but when I got over it, I looked back on it with fondness, happiness, and sentimentality.

*　　*　　*

Jordan had her sweet sixteen in a huge church auditorium a few weeks later. Savannah and I sat at a table together as we waited for the party to really start, although there were already tons of people turning up.

Jordan had people that reminded me of bridesmaids and ushers at her party. The names of these people were announced in pairs, a guy and a girl, by the DJ as they walked in to the center of the room and danced around a fancy white wicker chair. Everyone clapped as each couple made their way toward the chair for their turn to dance.

When Jordan was announced, the whole room erupted into a deafening chorus of cheers and applause. She entered with her date and sat proudly in the decorated wicker chair.

I couldn't believe what a ceremony it was! If I hadn't known any better, I'd have thought we were at a wedding reception.

Jordan told me a few days later that she thought the Spanish camera guy liked me. She said, laughing, "Yeah, the camera guy started at your ankles, then he went slowly up your legs, then up the rest of you before he zoomed in on your face!"

I hated it. I hated when older Spanish guys liked the way I looked. It grossed me out. First of all, I didn't really believe I deserved to be looked at in that way. It was too confusing. Was I ugly or gorgeous already? Why did I get two extremes from people so much?

Maybe it was just my body that was attractive, but people didn't like my hair and face. Admittedly, I had a really, really hot body. I knew this to be true because no one ever made fun of it. But hearing people compliment it made me feel bad about myself. What, did I look like a woman? Eeew. I wanted to look like a sixteen-year-old girl.

I didn't want to look like my mother. I didn't want to be my mother. Spanish men looked at her, too. And I hated the fact that people thought I was Spanish. Where I came from, Spanish people were seen as inferior and I didn't want to be dark. Horrible and racist as it was, that was how I felt. I was mostly Italian. *Italian,* not Spanish. I didn't want to be anything but white. This was fucking humiliating. My being dark and looking Spanish-like while my mother favored my snow-white, freckle-faced, blue-eyed red-haired sister. It was so unfair. People laughed at me and idealized her. I was a dork and she was cool. Unfair.

Chapter 14

Junior Year

The summer ended, and my junior year began. Those who had taken art for the previous two years now had a choice about the third year of our Regents sequence. We could replace one of our subjects with third-year art, and at the end of the year, we would then take an art Regents.

At first, I worried about it. Was I doing myself a disservice or depriving myself? In the end, I decided to drop math. I figured science, history, and Spanish were much more important than math, especially with how difficult it was and knowing I would never use it. I felt like a kid cutting class, but I did it anyway.

This year we had a real weirdo of a woman teaching science. She was kind of goofy and passive, allowing the class to make fun of her and be disrespectful. I'm sure it bothered her to an extent, but she didn't seem overwhelmed by it.

Our history course was taught by a new teacher named Ms. Jones. She was an attractive, intelligent, and assertive sort of person. Students, including myself, really liked her. She was quite different than the other teachers at Stella, including the fact that she was more progressive and feminist in her ways. Even though girls like Emma were in history, it wasn't too bad. No one really bothered me much. I'm pretty sure that was down to the excellent teacher.

We had Ms. Hernando as the new teacher in our Spanish

class. She was a little highly strung, but people respected her for it. She really knew her stuff and was consistent and disciplined in her teaching style. Caitlin would imitate her really well. "It's not 'poner'...it's *'po*-ner'!" she would say, slapping her own hand. There weren't really any of the popular girls in Spanish class. This year, I was determined to perform well in school and was paying particularly close attention in Spanish, so I actually really enjoyed the class.

For art, we had the same teacher from freshman year. Minnie and Mellie were in art again, so I was looking forward to having fun with them.

Gym was also with the same teacher, the sweet lady from freshman year, Ms. Rayfield.

For religion, we had a new nun named Sr. Jenna. She was a small, thin woman with hardly any hair. Masculine-looking on a good day, she was extremely smart and assertive with our class.

Then there was health class. It was a relatively small class in a non-traditional classroom on the first floor, with rows of long tables that stretched out in cramped lines across the center of the room.

I also took typing that year, which I found out was a good class, although I didn't see how I was ever going to learn to type. It had always seemed hard, and I had no idea how I was going to memorize where all those letters were. I could only do one key at a time, and that was only when I dared to venture close enough to a typewriter.

*　　*　　*

One morning, I walked up the sidewalk leading to the school building with a couple of friends. Isabella and Emma were a few feet behind us. "Wow, her hair looks great," I heard Emma mutter.

"What? Eeew." Isabella sounded repulsed by Emma's comment.

I knew they were talking about me.

"It *does*...and last year she looked like such a slob."

Wow. What a compliment.

I felt hurt, of course, but there was a part of me that felt good. To actually get any sort of compliment from one of these girls really spoke volumes to me.

A brunette named Amelia joined our crowd that year, basically because she liked Jordan, India, and Bella. Amelia wasn't very nice to me most of the time. She could be somewhat insulting to me. Savannah also seemed to be on the receiving end of negativity from her, which kind of made me feel better to know I wasn't the only victim. Amelia certainly wasn't in our group to hang out with Savannah and me.

One of the first mornings of junior year, I was called down to the auditorium by one of the vice principals. When I arrived, I found the vice principal standing with a tall, pretty girl I'd never seen before. She had black hair, Guidette-style so it kind of stood up to the ceiling, and the longest nails I'd ever seen in my life.

The vice principal introduced Josephine to me, and I was asked to take her around school that day. I was surprised but very flattered that out of all the girls in school, I would be asked to do this by the vice principal. Josephine would be in my homeroom, which was probably part of her logic, but still.

As she and I walked around the empty hall, Josephine told me a bit about herself. Apparently, she had her own mansion, her own Ferrari, and her own hair salon.

Okay, the car I could see, but her own hair salon? And for God's sake, did she expect me to believe she lived on her own? The girl was a junior, so she had to be no older than sixteen. I didn't know what to do with this new information; it all sounded so foreign to me. I tried to process her story as we walked.

It became clear this girl was strange, strange territory. The feeling I had around her was the same feeling I'd had in freshman year, when I thought of girls my age already having serious relationships, sex even. That feeling of knowing they were older, more mature, and knew more about life than I did. Josephine had the same effect.

I introduced her to my friends in homeroom, and she quickly settled down in the back with us. In fact, she sat right next to me.

As I invited her to sit with us at lunch, I had a feeling—and a fear—that Josephine was the kind of girl who would soon ditch us and move on to "better things" like the one from summer school had. In fact, Savannah kept raising the same concerns, but it was too hard for me to hear so I brushed it off.

As time went on, Josephine confirmed our predictions to be correct. She became less and less enthusiastic about us and frequently stayed in her seat without saying a word to any of us.

*　　*　　*

Unfortunately, I had a bit of a hard time in English class. While it wasn't all that frequent, the times the popular girls did decide to pick on me, it was horrible. At times, it was even done in front of the teacher, who did nothing to stop it.

A couple of the girls who bothered me in English were Nicoletta, the miserable, mean, angry best friend of Isabella's, and Maria, the girl who'd hated me since freshman year. Although there were others, those two were the worst. I hated both of them, but Nicoletta was the one I was most afraid of.

Angelica the god, Isabella, a friend of theirs, and a few others were all in my religion class with me. One time, the popular girls were ridiculing and insulting homeless people. Angelica the god said to the class, "I saw the homeless man so I went over and gave him a dollar like this..." She then demonstrated how she'd handed him the dollar with one outstretched arm while keeping her head turned away from him and wrinkling her nose. Her pose was one of disgust, not kindness. Her friends, however, all thought it was hilarious.

Gym, as always, was a big class, so there were plenty of the popular girls to go around, including Tanya, Angelica, and some others. Fortunately, I had a good number of friends, like Bella and Caitlin, in the class too.

I enjoyed spending time with my friends in art, but there was another girl called Amy who also sat with us. She liked Minnie and Mellie but didn't seem to like me. Like with Amelia, Amy certainly wasn't sitting at our table to be with me.

*   *   *

One school morning, I stood waiting near my house for the bus when I saw a girl in a freshman uniform with curly shoulder-length hair. I think about three girls who went to Stella lived in my neighborhood. We smiled and said hi to each other. After that, we saw each other every morning and took the buses together to school. Talking most days and quickly forming a friendship, it seemed clear we liked each other a lot. Her name was Katrina.

It turned out Katrina had been friends with a boy in our neighborhood who had passed away a few years before. He had dehydrated and collapsed. To me, his death had been very disturbing as I'd never known someone dying at the same age as me. I never knew the kid personally, but the fact he had lived in our town was close enough.

In addition, Katrina shared with me that her father had passed away suddenly only months before. I felt really terrible for her;

I couldn't even imagine what that must've been like for her. Whenever I thought of her or associated with her, that was the first thing I would remember. However, Katrina seemed to be very strong and centered. She didn't appear fragile about her father's passing; it was as though she'd put it behind her.

Katrina had a friend named Jean, also a freshman. She was talkative and known for sometimes irritating people, Katrina included.

At times, I got the feeling that Savannah was jealous of my getting closer to Katrina. I wasn't sure, but it made sense. It was true that I was becoming closer to her, but I was also drifting away from Savannah.

Savannah and Jetta made comments that my new freshman friend followed me around like a "puppy dog." I ignored them, but that's when I knew for sure they were envious.

Katrina told me that Jean kissed my ass all the time. As flattered as I was, I was also disappointed. I thought I was becoming liked by really cool people. I didn't want my ass to be kissed. That wasn't how I wanted to be liked. Jean was only responding to behaviors that made me appear cool, behaviors that I'd learned from the popular girls in my year. Because Jean wasn't in my year, she just assumed that's how I was. She didn't know my real status. In some ways, I started devaluing her friendship, but there was a part of me that liked being this popular, even if it was only with one person.

*　　*　　*

As the fall went on, Bella's father was taken ill and he unexpectedly passed away. His death had a really weird effect on me, and it somehow intensified my attachment to Bella.

I'd never had any idea of what to do or say to a person after they'd lost a loved one, so I turned to Katrina the next morning for advice, seeing as she'd lost her father too. As we waited for the bus to school, she was telling me things like, "Just remember, don't force her to talk about it if she doesn't want to, just let her talk about it in her own time."

Her words really hit home and stuck with me for a long time. Not only that, Katrina herself hit me and stuck with me too. She'd had such a strong impact on me in the little time I'd known her; I didn't know why, but there was just something about her. I had no clue how to deal with Bella's situation, but what Katrina said sounded like words of huge wisdom. It almost felt like she, or maybe even God, was speaking exactly of my tendency to force people to talk about something they didn't want to, purely for my own needs.

A few days later, I went by bus to the funeral home where the wake was. Wakes had always freaked me out. I hated seeing a dead person right in front of me. The whole thing always confused me, and I'd often feel physically weird afterwards.

I'd never really gotten a good look at Bella's father—I'd only ever seen the back of his head when he drove us home—but there he was. A somewhat thin man, with dark skin like the rest of his family.

Bella held up really well. I didn't see her cry once, but I figured she'd done her share of weeping already. If anything, she was her usual self—a pisser, laughing sometimes. In response, even I was able to be myself since the family was up for laughs too.

After the wake, my father came to pick me up. As he approached the building, he said, "I'm going to the pizza store. I'll be right back."

When Bella asked where my father went, I said, "He's gone to the pizza store."

"Pizza store?" she replied with a puzzled look on her face. "It's a *pizzeria!*"

"Oh yeah! You're right," I said, laughing.

"Pizza store," she repeated, imitating my father using a silly low voice.

When Bella's cousin came out and saw I was still there, she asked, "Where's Mary's father?"

"He's at the pizza store," Bella and I said in unison. Both of us cracked up laughing, but Bella's cousin had no idea what we found so funny.

After I left, Bella and the whole wake thing spun around and around in my mind. It hurt. I had to babysit that night, and I remember being at the house with the events of the day whirling round in the back of my mind when dealing with the kid, then very much in the front of my mind after she went to sleep.

After the kid had gone to bed, I stood in the kitchen staring at the phone. I needed to talk to Bella to see how she was doing. I called their home, no answer. I called again, no answer. Half an hour later, I called again. Still no answer. I knew they were probably either still at the funeral home or out together as a family. What am I doing? I thought. They need to be together right now, this is so inappropriate! But I refused to listen to my own reasoning.

I wanted attention. I wanted to be liked. So I took advantage of the situation. I cared about Bella, loved her even, but I also felt she deserved a lot of support from everyone. It was an opportunity for me to mark my territory, to make it known that I was Bella's "close friend."

To further my efforts, I wrote a poem dedicated to Bella's father. It was to be read over the P.A. that Monday morning, mainly as an announcement that her father had passed, but also to mark my territory, to support Bella, to get Bella's love, and to make myself look good.

As I think about you and all the time that we shared
I eventually realize that you really did care.
As I think about the special times that we had
I regret the times that I would get so mad.
All the times that we'd fight, all the times that we yelled,
They seem so foolish,
But at least I can tell
That our fights mean one thing
And that stands out clear
That you loved me and knew me
And I hold the days dear
When we would walk, when we would talk,
And even when we fought for weeks.
Now tears roll down my cheeks.
I wish you were here now to tell me what I'm feeling.
But you can't...you're gone.
And as I stare at the ceiling
I realize that without you a piece of me is gone too.
Maybe it's my heart. Maybe it went with you.
Now as I think about you I feel the pain in my heart flee.
Because as I glance in my mirror
I see your reflection in me.

Maybe it was a bit corny. When I wrote that poem I knew it was a poem that emanated from my own issues, no matter how lovely the gesture might have been. I didn't know anything about Bella's father or her relationship with him, nor had I heard of any fights they'd had. Deep down, I knew I didn't have a clear picture of what she was feeling.

Chapter 15

On Monday morning, I went to our principal, Sr. Agatha, to tell her what I wanted to do. One of my freshman friends went with me for support. Sr. Agatha got annoyed and said that, even though deaths and "keep in your prayers" were announced for relatives of students, what I wanted to do wasn't normal. She explained that other students might wonder why they didn't get that sort of treatment.

I understood what she was saying, but I assured her that I would resolve the issue by generalizing to other students as well. Plus, it wasn't as though the school itself was doing anything in favor of one particular student, it was another student who'd asked permission to do it. It wasn't exactly my fault that other students hadn't thought of a poem for their friend or weren't brave enough to put themselves forward to do it.

She then said to me, "Well, see Sister Jenna. She's in charge of morning P.A. prayers." Sr. Agatha seemed unconvinced what I was doing was a good idea. I was hurt by her reaction. There I was with a lovely poem I'd written and wanted to share—hard enough for anyone, let alone a teenager—yet I'd been shamed.

Mildly upset, I went with my freshman friend to see Sr. Jenna, who was my religion teacher that year. "Bella Rodríguez's father passed away, she's a close friend of mine..."

"Oh, I'm sorry," Sr. Jenna said.

"And I wanted to know if it was okay if I read a poem on the P.A. this morning dedicated to her and her father."

"Oh, sure," she said with compassion in her voice. I felt better, but also even more angry now at Sr. Agatha. Sr. Jenna was okay with my idea, so what was the matter with her? Bitch.

Sr. Jenna said I might want to generalize it to other students. "Definitely," I replied emphatically. "That's what I wanted to do anyway."

So, shortly after speaking to Sr. Jenna, I went ahead and did it. I found myself in the main office in front of a microphone, with the paper in my hand. I announced his passing, and dedicated the poem to Bella, her father, and all students at Stella who had lost a parent or loved one.

I was immensely proud of myself. Who in their right mind was going to pick on me or hate me after that?

After I quietly left the main office to go up to my homeroom, I felt a sudden rush of depression wash over me. I felt badly for Bella. I also wanted attention, to be noticed. So, as I walked into my homeroom, I made sure to demonstrate how depressed and upset I was through my facial expression and my slow, mournful walk. Admittedly, I was being dramatic, but I did it well and I think people bought it. It wasn't like I was totally lying.

Anyway, I got compliments all day. When Sr. Agatha saw me, she smiled and shook her head. "Mary, how could I have ever doubted you?"

Of course, her words confirmed any positive thoughts I'd had about my overall performance that morning. I felt good about myself.

The part of the day that shocked me more than anything was when I was sitting on the bleachers in the empty gym after school. Who stuck her head in through the doors with an enthusiastic smile? None other than Britney Anderson. "Mary," she squealed. "Your poem was so good!"

I couldn't afford to say "Go fuck yourself," so instead, I pleasantly thanked her.

"Oh my God, I felt so bad. Is she all right?" she asked.

"I'm sure she'll be fine." We exchanged a few more words before she said goodbye and left.

Wow. Britney Anderson was just nice to me! And my predictions came true. Ever since that morning, the teasing and abuse I received, although it still happened occasionally, was never as intense again. I felt I'd gained a new-found respect from people—or at least some respect, or partial respect, or crumbs of respect—either way, it was much more respect than I'd ever had from these girls before.

*　　*　　*

One Saturday night not long after the funeral, I was walking around Howard Beach with my junior friend Diane. A strange rebellious feeling had me behaving differently than how I usually did. As we walked, I got a sudden urge to have alcohol. I wanted to be bad. When I brought up the idea to Diane, she said that her parents had alcohol at home—and they were out.

When we got back to her house, Diane showed me where the alcohol was in her parent's dining room set. She said it was "Vermouth" wine. We took it up to her bedroom and started drinking. I had no idea what it was going to feel like to have alcohol in my system.

Although the wine tasted more like vinegar at first, I soon got used to it and started to feel quite giddy. I called Minnie, my eccentric friend, and we had a hilariously funny conversation while Diane sat on the bed laughing.

After I got off the phone with Minnie, my feelings of happiness started to increase, and I couldn't stop talking to Diane. Except I wasn't really talking to Diane, I was kind of talking at her. "Mary, you're drunk!" poor Diane shouted, laughing.

Then something very strange happened. I started crying. I thought about Bella's father's death and how cruel it was that someone's parent could just die like that, not to mention how hard it had been on me, too. I cried and shouted about how much life sucked. As I banged my fist on Diane's bedroom wall, I tumbled off the bed and fell on the floor.

When I got back up, I noticed Diane was gone. "Diane?"

I wandered slowly down the quiet hallway outside her room. Everything was blurry. "Diane?" I called again. At the end of the hallway, I could see her bathroom door was slightly open and the light was shining through the gaps around the frame.

"Diane?" I whispered, knocking lightly on the bathroom door before pushing it open. A blurry figure with big hair was sitting on the toilet, slumped over and crying. It was Diane. I knew then that I'd upset her.

Later that evening, Diane went downstairs to greet her parents when they arrived home. I followed her downstairs, careful not to trip on the two stairs I was seeing with each step, and came face to face with her father at the bottom. He grinned slightly. "Feeling under the weather?" he asked. I really had no idea if Diane had told them about the wine or if she'd just said I was sick. Without any form of questioning, he drove me home with Diane in the car in silence.

When I got home, I burst through the door. My parents weren't home, but I saw my sister sitting in the living room. She looked concerned after I muttered something to her on my way to the phone to call Savannah. As soon as she answered, she said, "Mary.

I don't think I should be talking to you right now."

Slamming the phone back in its cradle, I then grabbed my coat and stumbled over to Jodi's house down my block. I stomped up the stairs to her house, rang her bell, and waited by the door.

Jodi finally appeared in the doorway and said, "What? What?" It seemed as though she knew something was wrong.

After I'd told her everything that was going on, she kindly offered to come back with me to my house. We went to my bedroom and she helped me get undressed, laughing and joking about how she had to help me take off my bra. I lay down in bed and she sat at my side while I cried and talked about all my issues. At one point, I said I wanted to think and feel like I was special.

Jodi tried her best to help me and jokingly reassured me I was special. "Trust me, Mary. You are special...very special," she said, laughing. I knew she meant it in a negative way, implying I was a weird or crazy kind of "special."

As she was leaving, she laughed again and said, "Never forget, Mary...I took off your bra."

Normally, Jodi tended to be very sarcastic and condescending. She was an all-round unhappy person. Katrina, after hanging out with the two of us once, told me she didn't like Jodi because she treated me poorly and was too insulting and critical of me. But, by then, someone insulting and criticizing me was something I just accepted. I never even considered that the mean person was wrong or that I was being treated badly. Whatever people said about and to me, I thought was true, justified, and warranted.

After that night, I vowed never to pick up a drink again. Getting drunk, alcohol, dizziness, blurred vision, headaches; the whole thing was all completely awful!

*　　*　　*

A couple of weeks later, a senior came up to our table to tell us something. We almost began a friendly conversation, but then it became apparent she was friends with Isabella. Isabella strode up to us and pointed at me, saying to the senior, "She called me an asshole last year."

"What?" the senior shrieked, glaring at me. If looks could kill, I would've dropped dead on the spot. I just turned away and sat down at our table.

One time, I was hurrying through the crowded halls between classes when I accidentally stepped on someone's foot behind me. "Sorry," I said.

"You'd better be," came the reply.

I turned and saw it was that senior, Isabella's friend.

I don't remember what had triggered it, but Isabella had started bothering me again, even in my homeroom. I went alone to Ms. Morris, our homeroom teacher, and informed her I was being targeted by Isabella. Other than that one time with Sr. Agatha, I'd never been to a teacher to "tattle," but I couldn't take it anymore. It was more painful with Isabella because we'd been quite friendly the year before.

Isabella found out I'd gone to Ms. Morris and sought her revenge in homeroom one morning. She started off by shouting something nasty at me in front of everyone, and then accused me of something ridiculous like what I'd called her the year before. I didn't shout, but I denied what she said and pointed out that she'd started the whole thing. Everyone was watching our argument with great interest.

Ms. Morris overheard the bickering and rushed up to us. "Okay, okay! Let's go outside," she said, ushering us toward the door.

I was so glad we were going to be alone. With Ms. Morris present, and Isabella therefore unable to hurl any more abuse at me, maybe we could settle things.

The three of us stood in the quiet hall as I told Ms. Morris, in front of Isabella, exactly what was happening. I went over the details of how Isabella was treating me lately, including the false accusations she'd been shouting across homeroom. I tried to emphasize to both of them that I'd never said anything bad about her, not intentionally anyway. The argument went back and forth between us with lots of finger pointing and various mentions of "she did this" and "she said that." Ms. Morris looked on in dismay.

Isabella even accused me of not handling the bullying very well, to which I replied, loudly, "Well, what would you have done if you were me? What would *you* have done, Isabella? That's the big question!"

Isabella seemed taken aback as she looked away and stuttered, "I don't know, I..."

Ms. Morris eventually interrupted and gave her own speech, which was good and calming for me to begin with. But then she also said, "Now, I don't know what happened last year, but..." The words "last year" triggered a feeling of trauma inside me.

Ms. Morris was done. She concluded by telling us she wanted no more teasing from Isabella and no more arguments in homeroom from either of us.

As Ms. Morris opened the door, I marched in first and quickly returned to my seat in the back of the room. When I looked up to the front, I saw Isabella smirking and snickering with people on her side of the classroom. It seemed as though a confrontation with me was as much of a joke as anything I had to say about it.

Afterwards, Nicoletta, Isabella's best friend, muttered cruel things to me throughout English class. Even though I had little hope for Nicoletta, I wanted to make peace. So, as soon as the bell rang and everyone got up, I went straight over to her desk.

Instead of hearing me out and trying to settle the problem, she angrily belittled me. "You called Isabella, *my* friend, an asshole. And the reason I bother you is...it's only because I don't like you, Mary. Most of us don't." Her voice and her words were bitter. I felt like I was talking to a dangerous dog that could bite at any second.

She threatened, "If you *ever* say anything about Isabella again, I'll kick your ass."

I wasn't afraid anything would happen to me physically, but I was afraid to say what was really on my mind. The need to stand up for myself overtook my fear, even if it wasn't the smart thing to do.

So I scoffed at her and said, "Yeah," as though she were a joke, and started walking away.

"Oh, what, you think I won't? You actually think I won't? *I'll have your head*!"

For someone in my position to utter even a syllable of defiance to one of these girls was huge and bound to bring on severe trouble. Basically, I was dealing with the mafia. Obviously, these girls weren't the mafia, but most of them had the same mentality.

After school that day, I was waiting for the bus home with Katrina. There were no other girls from Stella around because we had left the school later than normal.

Suddenly, I heard an angry yell from afar. "Mary!"

I looked down the Boulevard and saw two girls sticking their heads out of a car window several blocks away.

"Mary! You slut! You sluuuut!" one of them yelled.

Immediately baffled, I had no idea why they were now calling me a "slut." Had they come up with a new name for me just to get me in trouble in some other way? Did they want to give me some other kind of rep?

A part of me liked it. To me, being seen as a slut was much better than being seen as a geek or a loser. Plus, I was with Katrina, so I didn't want her to see them teasing me. I wanted her to think I was cool. I wanted her to admire me, which I had a feeling she already did.

Further in my favor, these girls were yelling in an angry, furious manner, as though I'd done something hurtful to them. As sick as it was, I felt that was more respectful.

So, ensuring that Katrina could see it, I smirked, laughed, and held my middle finger right up in the air. That got them screaming so loud it might have sounded like I was stabbing them had we not been several blocks apart. "Slut! You slut!" they continued.

In school the next day, much to my relief, nothing horrible happened as a result of my showing off at the bus stop. Maybe it was because they weren't "allowed" to bother me anymore, although Isabella and her friends would sometimes say things as they passed like, "Ms. Morris, help me! Help me!"

Anyway, the "slut" thing didn't last very long.

Chapter 16

When I first saw the movie *Goodfellas*, I couldn't believe my eyes. The way the mob insulted other men who weren't "with them" captured perfectly how I was treated at school. Oh my God! I thought. This is too familiar. It was hard for me to watch. They were male versions of these girls. Other than for the absence of the physical violence, the mentality and behaviors were exactly the same.

At times, I noticed I took on traits from those around me and my environment as a whole. My parents were verbally and emotionally abusive during my childhood and adolescence. My father was physically abusive, too. Despite their behavior, they didn't seem to show any guilt or remorse for their actions.

Fortunately, my father's violent tendencies began to decrease over time. Academically, I told myself over and over that things would be different for me that year, too. I would work my butt off. And I did. My grades improved so much I was getting scores in the eighties and no longer failing.

Like the popular girls, I learned to tease, bully, and turn people against others. Usually, the only people I'd pick on weren't much of a threat in the first place. The biggest difference, however, was that I experienced guilt and was aware that what I had done was wrong. Not that it was an excuse, but it certainly distinguished me from the popular girls.

I was also picking on Savannah. I didn't want people to like her. It wasn't too hard to accomplish because people didn't like her anyway, either because she was weirdo-geek, or because she could be bitchy sometimes. Or a combination of both.

Strangely, I loved Savannah at the same time. It truly was a love-hate relationship.

It was around this time when I started doing my hair down, with a tiny ponytail thing on the top right side of my head. It was a popular style back then, but the way I had mine looked silly and people sometimes made fun of it. For example, a girl once said in Earth science class, "Shut up, Mary Powell, or I'll cut that little thingy off the top of your head." Laughter consumed the class. As usual, I just took it and never retorted back. I couldn't; I was too paralyzed with fear and embarrassment.

There was another girl, Dina, who got it almost as bad as Savannah and I did. She always said whatever came to her mind and invariably made other people angry. They attacked and verbally abused Dina every time she opened her mouth, but it didn't distract them from making fun of me and Savannah.

One time, I took the bus into school instead of the train. I was alone in the packed bus, and Dina happened to sit next to me. She was her usual snobby and rude self, so I started snapping at her. After all, it was safe to give it back to her.

"No-life!" I called her and looked out the window.

"You're a no-life!" she responded and started complaining to other girls around her. For whatever reason, they'd suddenly decided they weren't abusing Dina now. "She's not popular, and she's saying..." That's all I heard before she stood up and continued to ramble on about me to the other girls.

Later, in homeroom, I overheard one girl say, loud—most likely for my benefit—as she got the story from Dina, *"Mary Powell* called *you* a no-life?"

When it came down to it, even the most abused and ridiculous girls seemed to be favored over me. It was confirmation that people really didn't like me.

*   *   *

Blue and Gold came round again. Back on the gold team again this year, I knew I was going to do a good job in dancing. Unfortunately, in comparison to the other team, our aerobics team was weak. Blue team won aerobics in the end, as well as several other categories.

Our dance performance on the first night was outstanding. We looked striking dressed all in black, and everyone wore a black baseball cap with their hair sticking out the back in a ponytail, just like Janet Jackson did. The choreography was awesome, and we took an easy win on the first night. However, the second night, we lost.

When blue was announced the winner for dance on the Friday night, virtually the entire left side of the gym, consisting of the gold team members and fans, started chanting, "Bullshit! Bullshit! Bullshit!" The gold dance team cheered up when it was announced we'd won overall, meaning we were the dance competition winners for the third year in a row. As much as dance queen Danielle got on my nerves, she was a great choreographer.

When the blue team were crowned overall winners for the entire Blue and Gold series, I was beyond depressed. Blue won? We lost? Blue and Gold meant a lot to me, probably more than to the average Stella girl. The depression lasted until the following night. I remember lying on the couch watching TV, too bummed even to cry, but as the night wore on, I started to feel better.

*   *   *

A few weeks later, I met a cute guy at an all-boy's school dance I'd gone to with Mellie and her friend. The three of us were just talking with him at first, but when he figured I was interested, he asked me to go into the hallway outside the auditorium with him.

We were pretty much alone in the hallway, and he kissed me right away. And then he started with his tongue. Gross. Disgusting. But again, I did it. I thought I had to do it as part of growing up, as part of being cool.

We kissed for a while longer, but then I told him I wanted to go back to the auditorium. We found Mellie and her friend sitting on the bleachers, and the four of us got into a conversation. I started talking excitedly about school, especially Blue and Gold. I noticed the look on his face, which suggested he was becoming increasingly irritated and bored. I guess he just wants to make out, I thought.

Shortly after, he made his excuses and left. I didn't know whether I'd made a hyper fool of myself talking so excitedly like a nerd, and about school for Christ's sake, or if I was fine and this guy was just a bastard who wanted to get laid. Something told me it was the latter.

Later on that evening, I saw one of Mellie's friends smoking. The more I watched her and smelled the cigarette, the more I wanted one myself. I couldn't believe I was thinking of smoking. Ever since my grandmother had died from emphysema, I'd been strongly against it. Nevertheless, when Mellie's friend saw my intrigue and offered me some of her cigarette, I reluctantly took a tiny puff from it. Much to my surprise, I liked it, so the girl gave me a full one of my own. Teenagers were allowed to smoke in the auditorium, so I proudly held my cigarette between two fingers—like I'd seen real smokers do—and I instantly felt "cool." Admittedly, I was also a bit shocked I was actually smoking.

*   *   *

Jordan and I were on our way out of the school building one day when we saw a sign for the upcoming cheerleading tryouts. She and I talked it over and decided to give it a go. The very idea of cheerleading at Stella got me so thrilled! I loved watching the cheerleaders at Blue and Gold, who always did a number after each team had performed. What I enjoyed the most about these cheerleaders was that they danced to choreography. Although my previous attempts had been a little shaky, I'd always wanted to dance well, and that only intensified my desire to become a cheerleader.

I went to the first tryout with Jordan where we first had to learn a couple of cheers as well as the postures that went with them. We also had to learn a full dance by memorizing it and then practicing it at home. At the next tryout, we each had to do cheers while the others watched, and then we did the dance as a group.

Because my parents' bedroom was bigger than mine and had a couple of mirrors, I used their room to practice my moves. I worked so hard that by the time the tryouts came around, I had every single step memorized. There had been a few moments of wanting to give up, but I'd forced myself to keep going. I'd wanted it too much to let my inhibitions get the better of me.

I remember being incredibly nervous the afternoon of the tryouts. We were in the auditorium and Jill, the head cheerleader, announced it was my turn to audition. I felt a little self-conscious to cheer and yell by myself, but I had no choice.

Encouraging myself to try to act confident, I did the cheer and each of the steps to the best of my ability, and I yelled "Okay!" just about loud enough for the whole school to hear.

We all did the dance in a group. Both Jordan and I did really well, and we both wound up getting in. I don't think I'd ever been as happy in my entire life. We were going to be cheerleaders in our senior year!

The Regents came and once again I passed everything, including a ninety-four in Spanish. I was so shocked but ecstatic at the same time. Me! A high score on a Regents test! I was so proud of myself. I also felt immensely grateful that I'd swapped math for art because there's no way I would've coped with another math Regents. Even better, because I passed all my Regents, I wouldn't have to take Regents tests ever again.

*   *   *

When the summer finally arrived, I could not believe I was going to be a senior when I returned. And I was so excited about the upcoming summer that I had with Katrina. We planned to hang out in the neighborhood the whole time. I was planning a fabulous year and I had more friends than ever.

During the summer, I began to take more notice of a guy, Nicholas, who lived across the street from me. He had always been there, but I'd never paid him much attention before. My mother had mentioned him to me a few times, not with any meaning, but I knew he was there. It came to my mind that maybe he was cute.

I found out that Nicholas was nineteen. I'd always thought he was a couple of years older than me; he looked it. In my mind, I knew I needed a guy to like, so I kind of made myself like him.

I had just obtained my driver's permit too. I'd studied for the test like crazy, unable to believe I was going to learn to drive. Like my father! My mother had never driven. I was so used to her not driving that the very thought of her behind a wheel was weird.

I did great on the written test and came out with an almost perfect score. When I got home that afternoon, I saw Nicholas by his house across the street. I took a quick glance at him, curiously, then quickly looked away.

A couple of days later, I was leaving my house one evening and I heard, "Hey." I looked across the street and could see it was a male, but I couldn't make out whether or not it was Nicholas. Holding a cigarette to his mouth, he stared at me. I ignored him, long since being used to guys cat-calling me. Ignoring was what I typically did. I just got used to taking it.

I never found out who cat-called me that night. It might've been Nicholas, but it could've easily been someone else who lived there. I knew Nicholas had an uncle who lived with him, along with his parents. Nicholas was an only child.

As it became warmer and I spent more time outside, I began to exchange sneaky glances and smiles with Nicholas, until one day he finally came across the street to talk to me. My heart pounded like crazy; I was so nervous, yet so on a high.

We had a short, friendly conversation, and then he went back across the street to his house. Maybe he likes me, I thought—or he *will* like me!

From then on, I was obsessed with him. Whenever I was home, I'd constantly be looking out of any of the front windows of our house that gave a view of across the street. I never missed an opportunity to see him go outside or arrive back home. I would get on a high whenever his large grey car with black leather attached to the front pulled into the driveway.

Nicholas was Italian. His parents were from Italy. He was a "Guido," as these guys were often called back then. His car was a "Guido-mobile," with Nicholas' Italian ribbons of red, green, and white hanging off the mirror. That was the in thing for cars.

A couple of weeks into summer, I found out that Nicholas had a girlfriend, this Guidette girl named Priscilla. Although this probably should've discouraged me and made me back off, it only made me more determined to make him mine.

Every time I left Katrina's at night, I'd feel a rush as I walked from her place, down her block, and toward the corner where I'd turn left onto my block. My insides tied into knots as I neared the corner, wondering if I might see him or his gray Guido car that I loved.

Sometimes, I'd see him by his house, in which case I'd sit on my porch and wait for him to come over to talk to me. He'd occasionally talk about his girlfriend. In truth, I was always hoping to hear they'd broken up because he'd fallen madly in love with me. But I never did.

Although none of my friends understood why I liked Nicholas—they all thought he was ugly and often called him "chipmunk"—he was always on my mind. Whenever I hung out with Katrina in the neighborhood, he was constantly in my thoughts. I think I drove Katrina mad with saying "he lives around here!" and "I could see him at any second!"

Nicholas' uncle, in his forties probably, also became friendly with me, my sister, and Katrina. He was kind of a pervert and was always talking about sex, really inappropriately. But I didn't think there was anything wrong with that; to me this was just how guys were supposed to be.

Nicholas called me out of the blue one day. I couldn't believe it. He asked what I was doing, and I said I was going to be hanging with Katrina and another friend.

"Oh, okay," he replied. "I was going to ask you if you wanted to hang out, but you're going out..."

My heart was thumping. Oh, man! "We can hang out!" I said, perhaps a little too enthusiastically.

"No, no. You're going out. Go out with your friends."

I was so disappointed and instantly wished I hadn't said I was busy. It felt like a once-in-a-lifetime opportunity. We'd been friends for several months by that time and he'd never asked me to hang out before. What if he never asked me again?

When I went out that afternoon, I talked about it non-stop.

The next day, Nicholas was at my porch and we were talking. He said he was supposed to go out with his friends that night but that it wasn't going to happen. I held my breath and asked him if he wanted to hang out with me instead. He agreed, and we made plans to meet up later that day and see a movie.

Well, I was over the moon. The second he left, I raced around the corner to tell Katrina. She came to the door and I practically screamed it at her. "He said yes! He said yes!" Katrina was really happy for me.

Christy's father, who lived next door to Katrina, was outside and started teasing me in a childish voice. "He said yes! He said yes!" To hear someone else say it out loud only made me even more excited.

I hung with Katrina until it got close to evening, and then I went back around the corner to meet Nicholas. I waited for him by my porch.

And waited. And waited.

He never showed up. His car wasn't in his driveway so I knew there was no point asking for him at his house. After about two hours of waiting and feeling utterly devastated, I called Katrina. She ran around to my house to be with me and listened patiently as I vented about what an asshole Nicholas was. I was so angry and hurt.

We hurried to the front door when we heard a car pull up in front of my house. It wasn't Nicholas. Instead, we saw a guy hanging out the front passenger seat window, cat-calling me. "Hey, baby! You're so beautiful! You want to hang out?"

As I looked closely at this guy, I saw he was very cute. A little dark for my taste, perhaps Hispanic. I liked light-skinned guys and I really only wanted a white guy, but I decided to check it out anyway. Katrina and I sauntered over to their car and we started talking to them. The guy who yelled out to me was named Vinnie, and his friend's name, ironically, was Nicholas.

"Nicholas?" I asked, unable to hide the surprise in my voice. "I was supposed to hang out with a guy called Nicholas tonight, but he stood me up. Isn't he an asshole?"

"He stood you up?" Vinnie replied in disbelief, looking me up and down. "He's definitely an asshole." To hear another guy agree with me made me feel better.

Vinnie and I wound up exchanging phone numbers. I was glad, but of course Nicholas was still on my mind. Really, I'd only taken Vinnie's number because I was hurt and mad at Nicholas. But I soon decided I wanted a boyfriend, and screw Nicholas. He had a girlfriend anyway, so nothing was going to happen between us.

Vinnie and I talked on the phone and made plans to hang out the next day. Katrina was so happy for me, partly because she couldn't stand Nicholas and thought Vinnie was really cute.

The following day, I spent some time with Katrina and we discussed my forthcoming first date with Vinnie; she seemed as psyched out about it as I was. She came to the park with me, which is where I'd arranged to meet him, and we walked out past the playground toward the large hilly golf course beyond.

As soon as Vinnie arrived, Katrina said goodbye and left. Vinnie and I then started walking across the golf course and found ourselves all the way on the other side about twenty minutes later. We got to know each other and talked about a lot of different things, including school, family, and friends. I found out Vinnie was Italian, but kind of a hoodlum, as we called them. He dressed in baggy clothes—"homeboy" style.

I wasn't feeling very attracted to Vinnie, which I assumed was because I still wanted Nicholas. But I knew I should be attracted to Vinnie because of how cute he was. We made our way off the golf course and walked for about another hour or so toward where he lived in the next town over.

When we reached his house, we sat on his porch and talked some more until eventually, we started kissing. He made the first move. And here it was again, the tongue thing. Gross. Gross. Gross. I told myself, well, you better get used to this because this is how it is—this is what you have to do. I'd already been through it all before, so it should've been old news to me by then, but it wasn't. It was still gross.

At one point, he put his tongue in my ear, which I thought was weird; it tickled and made me feel uncomfortable. I really wasn't feeling anything for this guy. But I needed a guy, a proper boyfriend all to myself, and I couldn't have Nicholas, so I figured I was in no position not to go along with whatever it was Vinnie was doing— however weird it might be.

Vinnie then walked me to my house to take me back home. We were heading toward a park with a concrete baseball field, basketball hoops, and a playground. Right outside the park, on the sidewalk, I saw Nicholas. We were walking toward him. Vinnie had his arm around me. Oh my God, Nicholas was about to see me with another guy! I was glad. I thought it would make him jealous, and I was tired of humiliating myself by chasing after him. I wanted him to see I had better things to do.

He stared at us as we walked toward him. "Hi," he said. I said hi back but kept walking. My heart was racing. I thought about it the whole way home.

That night, I was sitting on my porch waiting for Nicholas to come home. As soon as he did, he slowly walked across the street toward me. "So who was that? Was that your boyfriend?" he asked.

Wow, he just called Vinnie my "boyfriend." I couldn't believe I had a boyfriend. At that moment, a mix of emotions swelled up inside me. I felt some disgust toward Vinnie; I didn't really want Vinnie, I wanted Nicholas! I remember thinking, Nicholas, you're right in front of me, talking about my so-called boyfriend, another guy, when the guy I want is you!

I plucked up the courage to ask Nicholas what had happened the other night when we were supposed to be watching a movie. He apologized and said something came up. I was still mad and hurt, but I decided to forgive him. After all, I was still so in love with him.

I had fun with Vinnie that summer, but Nicholas was constantly on my mind. I still did the checking and waiting for him thing whenever I had the chance. Vinnie knew nothing about my stalking of the guy across the street.

Chapter 17

It seemed everyone loved Vinnie, including my sister and Katrina. They thought he was cute and funny. Actually, he was very hoodlum-like, but that demeanor was "in" at the time. They said Vinnie was stylish and Nicholas was a "Guido."

Vinnie and I would make out—a lot. He did things to me physically I hadn't known about before. My parents hadn't told me about any of that stuff. Supposedly, a guy would "come" during sex. My sister had told me that, and that it was like a liquid. She said that she and her friends had watched a porn film as a joke and seen it happen.

Although I had no clue about these things, and although I was curious, I'd already decided I didn't want to do any of those things with Vinnie. Considering even just the tongue-in-ear thing freaked me out, the whole sex thing sounded gross.

Vinnie would sometimes take me down to his room in the house's basement. His sister would sneak us down there and then keep a lookout for their parents arriving home. One such day, Vinnie led me down to his bedroom, switched on some hip hop music, and turned out the lights. Due to his bedroom having no windows, the room instantly turned pitch-black.

As soon as we started kissing, he began feeling my breasts, first outside, then underneath my shirt. I felt very uncomfortable, but I thought it's just what I had to do with a guy. He took off my shirt and my bra, which left me feeling glad the lights were out—I felt extremely naked—but then he grabbed hold of my shorts and started to pull them off. That's when I got scared.

"No! Stop!" I yelled. I was really terrified. He stopped, and I made it clear I was not ready to go all the way. He said he understood, but I knew he wanted more and was going to try to get it. There was a part of me that did want to do it. I wanted to be the first of my friends to have sex. How cool would that be? I thought that, in order to be cool, you had to have sex and not be a virgin. In the end, I told Vinnie we'd do it, but in my own good time.

One day when my parents weren't home, Vinnie suggested we go to my parents' bedroom because they had a bigger bed. We lay down and fooled around for a while, and then he told me he was horny and "hard." I was just learning about all this new vocabulary, and that was apparently when a guy's penis grew longer and literally went "hard." He put my hand on it and said, "Help me out…Help me out."

Help him out? I guessed he meant he wanted me to satisfy him in some way. I really didn't want to touch him, and I wished he wasn't making me do this, but I said I would as long as I didn't have to touch it with my bare hands. I wasn't going to touch someone's privates—that would be really gross! So I told him to wrap a sheet around it. He did, and I felt a penis for the first time. Exactly as I'd been told, it was hardened and long.

Suddenly, he said, "Fuck the sheet!" and started to pull it away from himself. I refused to go anywhere near the actual thing, so I wrapped the sheet back around it and stroked it for a while. After no more than about a minute, I stopped. I wanted no more. "Are you done? That's it?" he said. He seemed angry for some reason.

"Yeah," I replied.

"Man, that's *fucked up* what you're doing!"

I had no idea what he was talking about. Didn't I just help him out like he'd asked me to? "You're an asshole," I said.

"Fuck you," he responded. "Why did you do that?"

"I thought I was helping."

"Oh." A look of understanding crossed his face. "Oh, okay." I guessed he thought I had teased him.

Vinnie and I experimented this way for several weeks, mostly in his bedroom. Gradually, more of our clothes came off and I reluctantly started to let him touch me in different places. Despite how much I didn't like it, I thought I had to just do it.

One day when we were in my bedroom, I decided I just wanted to do it. I wanted to have sex. I wanted to be cool. And Vinnie wanted it. He started educating me on oral sex, even though I had no intention of doing that.

"Oh by the way, if I start laughing after I come when you give me oral, that's normal. When a guy comes, a guy feels good!" I thought that was weird.

We stripped all our clothes off and lay on my bed.

I couldn't believe it. I was naked! With a guy!

I watched him put a condom on before he got on top of me and tried to put himself in me. As I felt the beginning of him start to go inside me, I suddenly realized I didn't want to do it anymore. I told him to stop.

But we'd done it! We'd had sex! I asked him for confirmation of that. He said he felt like he went in, so we'd definitely had sex.

I ran to the bathroom and wiped myself clean, and that's when I saw a spot of blood.

Unable to contain my excitement, I then went straight to the phone to call Bella.

"Yup, it popped," she said. I squealed with pride.

I wasn't a virgin anymore!

I went to meet with Bella that evening. As I was explaining every last detail of my encounter with Vinnie, my father showed up out of nowhere and insisted on driving me home. Bella knew I was in trouble. Feeling embarrassed, I sat in the car and watched as Bella laughed and drew her finger across her neck in a cut-off-your-head motion. I sat in the backseat, as I usually did, nowhere near my father. He accused me of attempting to have sex. Of course, I denied it.

"Well, I found this in your bedroom." He pulled out the condom and dangled it in front of me. I'd forgotten to remove it from my room!

"It isn't used," he said, "so I know you didn't do it." He meant that Vinnie hadn't come. Even though he clearly didn't know we'd really done it, he still proceeded to yell at me.

The minute I got home, I called Caitlin and I told her what I'd done with Vinnie. I eagerly awaited her response to my news.

Silence.

"Caitlin?"

"Oh my God, Mary, I dropped the phone. Now I don't want any more calls that are going to make me drop the phone!" She couldn't believe it; neither could any of my other girlfriends when I told them I was no longer a virgin. I didn't know what they really thought, but I was officially the female stud now! I'd had sex!

*　　*　　*

I was really curious about sex at the time, and I was telling Katrina and other friends every last detail about what was happening. I was like a guy bragging to his friends about his sexual escapades. That's what it was like for me. I was proud of it, and I loved the attention from my friends. None of them were with guys at the time and that made me stand out. I loved their jokes, including them teasing me by calling me a "slut." I loved it. What I did with guys became a conquest.

I still searched for Nicholas. Vinnie knew I had a friend named Nicholas, but he didn't know I was still very much in love with him. Nicholas and I would talk briefly about Vinnie during our short conversations on the porch but that would be it.

Savannah and Jetta got to meet Vinnie when he came over one time while I was with them. He only stayed for a short while, but as soon as he left, Savannah said, "On a scale of one to ten, he's a ten!" They thought he was so handsome.

Everyone loved Vinnie. Everyone but me. I just wasn't attracted to him. I knew I should like him, but he grossed me out more than anything. Partly, I thought, because he was dark and looked Hispanic. I just wasn't attracted to men of color. I wanted someone white. He was Italian, but he didn't look it.

It was the day before my seventeenth birthday. Katrina, Savannah, Jetta, Vinnie, and I thought it would be fun to stop by Stella to visit some people who were in summer school. We all stopped by the beach before going to school.

Vinnie still had his shirt off by the time we arrived at Stella, but he soon ended up with two nuns scolding him about being half-naked and telling him to put his shirt back on. Vinnie looked uncomfortable. He didn't know what to say. "Look, man..." he started.

"I think it's obvious that I am not a man!" one of the nuns replied with her arms folded across her chest.

While Katrina, Savannah, and Jetta found that hilarious, I was embarrassed. Didn't I know any better than to have my boyfriend in a school building with no shirt on?

Just as we were about to leave school, one of the assistant

principals saw us and started talking to us. The conversation turned to everyone's nationality and what we all looked like. I asked her what nationality I looked like, and I predicted she would say Spanish, which is what everyone usually said. She stared at me, then smiled and said, "Italian."

I was surprised and so happy. Finally! I was so sick of people thinking I was Spanish. I was ashamed of my dark skin and the fact that I supposedly looked anything other than Italian.

After we left, Vinnie and I waited for the bus alone right outside the school. As we stood there, I looked around the entire school to see if any of the popular girls were around, or anyone that might see I had a boyfriend—a cute boyfriend—and that I wasn't such a nerd after all. This felt like the perfect opportunity to get back at them for making me so depressed and angry. Unfortunately, I didn't see a single soul.

Vinnie took me home and I hung out in my room alone after he left. I had the radio on, and I was singing along to some songs, feeling incredibly excited about my birthday the next day. All day, I'd been wondering where the thrill and excitement was that I normally felt right before my birthday. It just hadn't been there at all. Now, it was coming. This was my time, and it was all about me.

*   *   *

In recent times, I'd been dressing rather suggestively. I saw nothing wrong with it and thought I looked great. Even other people, including my friends, complimented me on my nice body, but they would also make jokes about me dressing like a slut.

"Mary, where are your clothes?" Katrina joked once.

I was walking over the overpass street toward my house one day. I was wearing tiny denim shorts, which were rolled up to be even shorter, and a tight black tank top that was low cut and showing my stomach. Unfortunately for me, my father happened to drive by. I got an earful as soon as I got home about how I looked "cheap."

My mother had also said a few times that I dressed "cheap." Not only did I think this was really sexist of her but I also couldn't believe a supposedly liberal woman would say such a thing. Although there was a big part of me that knew my parents were right, I strongly believed it was okay to dress however I wanted. And my parents didn't stop me. To me, that was cool. And I loved it.

That little punk Jake passed by me one time with his friends and said, "If I give you ten dollars, will you give me a blow job?"

When I repeated to Bella what he'd said, she looked away in shock and mumbled, "Oh, shit!"

I felt ashamed by her reaction. I guess it was obvious to Jake, and now to Bella and probably the rest of the world, that I didn't have any money. I was humiliated.

I also told Vinnie what he'd said. Vinnie got up and said he was going to fuck him up.

"No, don't," I said.

"Come on! He deserves it!" Vinnie protested.

I still told him not to, but I thought, am I doing the right thing here? It was true, he did deserve it. Was I putting myself second?

After six weeks together, Vinnie and I went our separate ways. Despite Katrina's disappointment, a part of me was relieved to leave Vinnie behind.

Plus, I was on a quest to get Nicholas. He was all I could think of most of the time. Sometimes, I'd even get depressed over not being with him and my friends would have to comfort me.

I found out from Jodi's sister that Nicholas was a "real player," that he was "very Italian," and that he "liked his women strong." When I found out, especially that last part, I felt badly about myself.

I knew I didn't act strong around Nicholas, rather more like a love-sick little girl.

A week or so after I'd broken up with Vinnie, I decided to gather the courage to tell Nicholas I liked him. I couldn't take it anymore. I wanted him so much. So I sat on my porch one night and waited for him, waited to see him see me.

Eventually, he came home and walked over as soon as he saw me waiting. He stood and listened while I sat on my steps and told him how I felt.

I ended my speech by apologizing for telling him. "No, it's okay," he said. "I had a feeling."

He knew? Had I made a fool of myself? Did I look desperate and pathetic to him? I pictured myself waiting for him on my stoop, looking for him, watching every movement on the block, hoping it might be him. Maybe he knew it wasn't by accident that he'd seen me all those times.

After a few minutes, he told me he had to go. "Do you have any idea how hard it was for me to tell you how I feel?" I said, angry and disappointed. "And now you're just going to walk away?"

"Well, what did you want me to do? Rip your clothes off?" he asked calmly.

Yes! I thought. I wanted to be his girlfriend. I wanted him, and I wanted to get physical with him.

That was it. I sat in silence, unable to vocalize my thoughts, and he left without another word. I felt humiliated, but I didn't regret telling him. I'd needed to tell him; I couldn't hold it in anymore.

As the days passed by, my feelings for Nicholas got stronger. I'd come home sometimes and glance for black cars parked near his house—to see if Priscilla, his girlfriend, was visiting him. I knew her car because of the distinct skinny metal sign under the license plate, which read "Nicholas Loves Priscilla." It was very hard for me to constantly see her car parked by his house, solely because it was a painful reminder that they were still together.

Priscilla would often stay at Nicholas' for a certain amount of time during the day or in the evening. Katrina and I joked she was a "ho," who was only there so he could have sex with her.

*   *   *

While my main focus was very much on Nicholas, Vinnie and I still kept in touch here and there. Once, Katrina and I ran into him outside the pizzeria near my house. Vinnie got out of his car, and with him was a pretty girl. He kissed me as he said hello and chatted with me for a minute before going inside with the girl.

After we said goodbye, Katrina asked, "Are you all right?"

"What do you mean?" I asked.

"After what you just saw, aren't you upset?" Katrina sounded shocked.

"Why?"

"Vinnie was with another girl. He obviously has a new girlfriend!" Katrina said emphatically.

I hadn't even considered the idea that girl with him could be his girlfriend. I just thought she was maybe his friend or something. What was wrong with me? How had I not seen it? It had just gone over my head.

The weekend after I'd seen him at the pizzeria, Vinnie contacted me to tell me that one of his friends was having a Halloween party, and he asked me if I wanted to go. Of course I wanted to; I loved parties. The whole of Vinnie's crowd that I'd met over the summer would be there too. Although I was keen to accept his invitation, I still felt a little nervous about it. I knew it might be awkward with him and his friends since we were no longer together. But I still wanted to go.

So I went to the party, which turned out to be in a dark, crowded basement with loud music. One girl there asked me with sentiment in her voice, "Mary, are you and Vinnie going to get back together?" I don't remember what I said, but I probably bullshitted my way out of it somehow.

Vinnie drunk a lot of beer at that party, and later in the evening, we wound up sitting next to each other in a secluded area of the basement. Of course, we ended up making out. One side of me thought it was inappropriate because, weren't we broken up? But the other side was thinking, who cares? Have fun!

I had my first taste of beer that night. It was vile, but I forced myself to take a few more sips. After all, I had to learn to drink this stuff to fit in. I hadn't had a sip of alcohol in over a year, not since the Vermouth business.

Just before midnight, my father arrived to pick me up from the party. I could've died with embarrassment when Vinnie's friend announced in front of everyone, "Mary, your father's here!" I was seventeen years old and going home with my parent from a party! I knew everyone else was getting home in other, more grown-up ways. I felt so humiliated and like a loser, different from other kids as always.

My father had insisted that he be the one to take me home, and he'd reminded me at least a dozen times I wasn't allowed to go home with anyone from the party. Plus, I was used to my father driving me everywhere, so I wasn't going to argue with him. His violent, angry outbursts toward me were still going on, and I didn't need to give him any other reasons to snap.

I remember one of his outbursts in particular. My little brother and I got into a fight one time when we were home alone. Back then, I was at the point where I wanted to start practicing my punching skills for when I got into fights. I thought punching was the right way to fight.

Okay, here goes, I'd thought as I made a fist and took a swing at my brother. He ducked out of the way, but what I hadn't seen was my father walk in behind me as my fist flew through the air.

"I've just seen you try to punch him!" he yelled as he stormed into the room. "I saw you try to *punch your brother*!" He grabbed me by the arms, but I broke away.

My only thought was that I had to escape; I wanted to see Katrina. As I ran to the front door to get out of the house, my father stepped in front of me and blocked the door with his body. He sat down on the floor against the door, yelling at me that I couldn't leave. His terrifying stare bored into me as he glared at me from his place on the floor.

By the time I managed to escape through the back door, which my father obviously hadn't realized was unlocked, I was on the verge of tears and shaking. I walked around the block, got to Katrina's house, and rang her doorbell. She came out with a concerned look on face as soon as she laid eyes on me, and she gently put her arm around my shoulder.

The gesture made me uncomfortable and freaked me out. It was confirmation that there was truly a problem, and that there was something terribly wrong and outrageous about my family. We went for a walk and I told Katrina what had happened back at home. I felt ashamed and instantly regretted talking about it, because now it was out—my father was abusive, and I was different; we were different. I wanted my family to be a good, normal family.

As we walked toward the park, I told her with great difficulty some other things about what went on at my house. I felt so embarrassed.

"Yeah, I've heard things about your family," Katrina said.

Her words devastated me. I didn't want her to know the "bad" and "weird" things about my family, and it turned my stomach to know rumors were spreading around the neighborhood. To make matters worse, there was nothing I could do about it. I couldn't change them.

That punk Jake and his friends showed up in the park as Katrina and I sat and talked. They yelled things at us and teased us. Jake "accidentally" banged into me as he and his friends mooned us, actually *mooned* us, laughing.

I was horrified. Added humiliation and abuse. But I was too upset to do anything. I didn't even care as much as I usually did about stuff like that. I was too paralyzed with sadness at that moment, with tears streaming down my face.

We decided to leave the park since the little jerks were there. Jake and his friends yelled threats at us as we walked away.

"Oh, I'm really scared!" Katrina yelled. I couldn't answer them. And that made me feel like such a loser, knowing that I couldn't even stand up for myself.

Now it seemed Katrina was the one standing up for us. Wasn't I supposed to be the "tough" one? I didn't want her to see me vulnerable like that.

As we left the park and walked down the block toward my house, I saw my father.

"Hey!" he roared at the top of his voice. I could've heard him from back at the park.

He started to sprint toward us, and all I could do was watch in horror as the distance quickly closed between us. I was terrified of him. Katrina was getting to see firsthand how dysfunctional my family was and how my father was with me.

My father yelled at me to get back to the house. Katrina looked at me with fear in her eyes. "Do you want me to come with you?"

she asked gently.

"No," I replied. I couldn't let her see any more. I didn't want her to see the rest of whatever else was about to happen inside my house.

I don't remember what happened after Katrina left. All I know is we went home.

While my family was crazy and angry, I certainly wasn't totally innocent. Like many teens around me, I thought it was cool to stand up for myself, with as much aggression as possible.

One night, I was on my way to the bathroom before I went to sleep. As I passed my sister's bedroom, which was in darkness, I saw the outline of my mother sitting on the edge of my sister's bed. I could overhear them talking about me, and that's when I learned of one reason why my sister no longer bothered with me.

"She fights," my sister said.

"What do you mean, she fights?" my mother asked.

"She gets into fights," Andrea remarked in a critical voice.

Although I thought I was overhearing a private conversation, I couldn't help but wonder if my sister had heard my heavy steps approaching down the hallway and knew I was there outside the door. Maybe she'd said those words for my benefit.

Andrea's accusation did have a grain of truth to it, but I felt insulted, criticized, and rejected. Things were never the same between us after that. It never occurred to me to speak with her about what I'd overheard. In my family, it wasn't the done thing to resolve interpersonal conflict through discussion—at least not calmly, kindly, or effectively.

Chapter 18

Senior Year

I was sitting in the backseat of my father's car one sunny afternoon toward the end of the summer break. We'd been out somewhere and were on our way back home. Despite my feeling positive and excited about senior year, I suddenly burst into tears. My father glanced over his shoulder and asked what was wrong. Reluctantly, I went on to explain how my life-long career goal had been to become a teacher, or maybe a guidance counselor, so I could help people with their problems. But I'd realized that neither of those careers would make me much money. And I knew I couldn't become a psychiatrist because I didn't want to go to medical school.

I was in despair. I didn't want to live my life with little money like my parents had, although I didn't tell my father that part. My dream was to enter a career where I would make a good living.

Offering a potential solution to my conundrum, my father told me about what a psychologist was. He said it was like a psychiatrist, only I wouldn't have to go to medical school. I was thrilled to have discovered the answer to my future. I was going to be a psychologist. Why hadn't he told me about this before? Needless to say, psychology wound up being one of the subjects I took in senior year.

Also, I was going to be taking speed writing as well as typing this year. Home economics was another new class that I'd be attending. I didn't really know why I'd taken that class, especially considering my mother had said it was sexist, but I did, and I was excited about it. The main source of excitement was probably because several of my friends would also be there, including Bella, Jordan, Mellie, and Jodi.

Several of my friends were in this year's gym class too, but there were also going to be many other girls there who still scared me. Britney Anderson, Tanya, Nicoletta, Kitty, and many, many others. Twice a week, completely out of my control, I had to face these girls and be much closer to them than I would've liked. I was exposed to them under minimal supervision. There were at least thirty girls in the class and only one teacher. She had two helpers, but no one really paid much attention or bothered to intervene when it came to any social problems.

In my first home ec class, the teacher told us we were going to be using sewing machines to make either a bear or a Santa doll for Christmas. My friends and I chose to make the bear. Supposedly, this bear would be red and green and come out looking really nice as a gift for Christmas, but I struggled to envision how I could ever make an actual teddy bear—stuffed, sewed, and everything. My friends laughed at my self-doubt and seemed so confident in their own abilities, but me? That just wasn't my thing.

Homeroom was very much the same, with all the same friends. One day during the first week of senior year, Minnie said, "Anybody ever notice that every time Mary talks, everyone always pays attention?" That meant a great deal to me. It told me there was something about me, my voice, the way I spoke, that made people gravitate toward me and want to hear what I had to say. Wow, what a confidence boost that was for the start of the year.

A few weeks in, our homeroom teacher made an announcement that a girl from Italy would soon be joining us. Although the news was exciting, it was already obvious the Italian girl wouldn't be our friend; she wouldn't be in our group, I knew that. It was highly likely she'd become one of the popular girls.

While Katrina and I were becoming closer and closer, I was pushing Savannah further and further away. To me, she was a total geek who everyone laughed at, and she could be a real bitch at times. I'd made some better friends anyway. In fact, I'd made a ton of better friends. I loved walking around with a crowd, and I was often the one in the spotlight.

Every day, I'd make my way home from school with my big crowd of friends. We'd all take the train—my crowd dominated the train by running around, laughing, and yelling—then some of us would get off the train and take the bus together, then a few of us would get off the bus and take the next bus together. By the time I got home, my hair and clothes would be a total mess from all the running around.

As promised, the girl from Italy came to our class and was now part of our homeroom. Her name was Dolores, but we soon took to calling her "Dolly" for short. She was seated with us and we made the most of getting to know her better. We, especially me, became quite close with her during the weeks after she arrived. She was great—loud and a lot of fun.

However, she turned out to be another person in our group who became the center of attention. I loved Dolly, but I wanted to be the clown, the crazy and loud one. But my pangs of jealousy were there only some of the time and they went away completely after a while. I saw she was a whole different person than I was. She didn't take the spotlight away from me; she respected me and I continued to have my role. My friends and my role in the group were making my high school years wonderfully happy.

By that point, I'd become really close with Katrina and so many others, but I was still barely talking to Savannah. I knew she was jealous of the friendship I had with Katrina. In truth, I didn't care. One time, I even sat her down in the cafeteria and told her she was no longer my best friend, and that Katrina was my new best friend. I don't know why I felt the need to tell her; perhaps it was a sadistic cruel streak, or maybe I just wanted to be honest.

Savannah had a hurt and angry look on her face. It didn't bother me, I just wanted to get it over with. And it was only Savannah. No one liked her anyway. She disgusted me.

After that, we occasionally talked here and there, but it was never the same.

*　　*　　*

Boy, was I due to be busy that year. Between classes, I was applying to college, cheerleading, dancing with the hip hop team I'd joined, and going to the liturgy club I'd also just joined. I was going to be stressed.

In my head, I saw myself as a hip hop dancer, which was why I joined the new hip hop club at Stella, led by an African American junior named Felicia. I liked the girl. She was outspoken. Britney Anderson and her little friends had even said, "She always opens her mouth! She thinks she's Martin Luther King!" Racism showed its face in many different ways at Stella. Felicia didn't seem to like Britney Anderson either, which was another point scored in her favor.

At the liturgy club, we would take turns to read a prayer on the P.A. system during the first period of the day while everyone was in homeroom. The difference between me and other members was that I wrote my own prayers, and they were pretty damn good. They were personal and poetic. Admittedly, they were also too long. Katrina brought this to my attention when she said, "We were all listening to your prayer in homeroom, and people in my class kept saying, 'Amen! Amen! Amen!'" In other words, shut up already and finish! That didn't make me feel very good about my writing; I felt a little ashamed. I was told I had to shorten them. But that was typical me, always talking too much, revealing too much.

Dolly joined the liturgy club with me and so did Katrina, which was strange because Katrina identified herself as an atheist. I didn't understand Katrina for that. How could anyone be an atheist?

Outside of my school life, I still watched for Nicholas around his house. I still wanted him so bad.

"Mary, you look so horny," Katrina said to me one day, and she and Diane laughed. I told Diane and Katrina to go and ask Nicholas if he liked me, and then I went for a walk while Katrina and Diane completed my request. I was so excited but so scared. Truthfully, deep down, I didn't have a good feeling about it.

When I got back from my walk, Katrina had a sad look on her face. "I'm sorry," she said.

They told me he said he didn't feel the same way. I was crushed.

"We asked him if he thought you were pretty, and he said, 'Yeah, I think she's pretty, but she's not my type.'"

I felt so depressed. Was that all I was? Pretty? Pretty, but not good enough? Refusing to accept what he'd said, I decided I was still going to try.

I got a phone call that night; it was Nicholas. "Mary," he said, "if you have something to tell me, don't get your friends to do it."

"You really don't feel the same way I do?" I asked.

"No," he said.

"Can you come over? Please?" I practically begged.

"Come over?" He laughed. "But I'm all dirty."

"I don't care."

"You don't care? Okay, I'll be right there."

I was scared. Nicholas was coming over! This was it, I was going to make him mine. And the timing was perfect because my parents weren't home and my brother and sister were in their rooms.

As soon as he arrived, he sprawled out on my couch with a look on his face that suggested he didn't really want to be there. I didn't care; he was there, and I was happy to take whatever I could get.

I sat curled up on the couch, facing him. He slouched further down, looking away from me. I wanted to kiss him.

"Oh, what the fuck..." I said out loud before I put my lips to his. He immediately started tongue-kissing me back. I couldn't believe it. We were kissing. He did like me after all! But at the same time I thought, he has a girlfriend and he's doing this?

He started groping me a little. I realized I wasn't grossed out at the idea of touching him, not like I'd been with Vinnie. Placing my hand over his crotch, I slowly started touching him. I was so happy. I was so in love with him.

"You can go in, you know," he said.

Did he mean for me to go down his pants?

I did it anyway. I slid my hand under the waistband of his pants and started jerking him and kissing him some more. I wanted him to come; I'd never seen that before. After a while longer, he did. I put my head on his shoulder as he came. It looked like a grayish liquid. Beaming with joy, I ran to get him a towel and he cleaned up. Then he left, saying he would call me the next day.

The next day, I went to school early and couldn't wait to tell all my friends. There were already a few people in my homeroom when I arrived, including Caitlin.

"Hey, Mary. How's it going?" she asked.

I replied dreamily, "The best things could ever be!" Then I went into all the details about everything that happened between Nicholas and me.

Amelia came up to me in gym class later that day and shook her head. "Mary, why do people not like you so much in this school?" She spoke in a disrespectful, condescending manner, as though it were my fault people at Stella gave me a hard time. "Everyone is going around saying you're pregnant."

I couldn't believe it. Well, me and my big mouth. After all, I had told Caitlin all about the previous night while other people were around. It was my fault.

As our gym class went outside, one of the popular girls asked me in front of the entire class, "Are you pregnant, Mary Powell?"

"No!" I scoffed and turned around.

Thankfully, that was it. That was the end of the rumor. I guess my saying "no" to the bitch's question had done the trick.

After rushing home from school that day, I waited and waited for Nicholas to call me. When he didn't, I figured maybe he wasn't home and decided to call Katrina to hang out instead. As we walked down my block, I was venting to Katrina about Nicholas when a car pulled up next to us. Two girls leaned out of the window and said something while laughing and pointing at us.

Then I saw someone sitting in the back seat of their car. It was Nicholas. He had his hands over his face, as though to say, "Oh shit, get me out of here."

They drove off. I couldn't believe it. He'd been sitting back there like it was some kind of big joke. Like he didn't want to see me, and we'd only been fooling around the night before. I felt stupid.

I called Nicholas up later that evening, and he apologized for not having called me. "I have a girlfriend," he said, "I've been with her four years. We can't be together!"

It hurt. I wanted him to say he wanted me. I wanted to try one more time to see if he liked me; I just couldn't, wouldn't believe he didn't. "Is there anything else you want to say to me?" I asked.

"Yeah...You have nice breasts."

I have nice breasts? Wow, I thought. At least that made me feel good about how I looked. Yet he wasn't giving me what I needed. He didn't want me. In fact, he'd just insulted me.

When I told Caitlin about the breast comment, she said, "Oh my God!" in disgust.

I was immediately concerned that Caitlin would now dislike Nicholas even more. I wanted her to like him; I wanted her and everyone else to think he was a good guy, and I didn't want anyone else telling me otherwise. All I did want, was Nicholas.

At lunch the next day, I sat at Bella's and Jordan's table, with India, Amelia, and Jodi. Jodi was already strongly against Nicholas; she knew of him and how he was. She lectured me in a condescending way, in front of everyone, about how I was making a big mistake pursuing him.

"You deserve better!" she said.

"Yeah," I replied, sighing. "But what I want to know is, what is better? I'm in love with Nicholas. What could be better than that?" Everyone remained quiet. No one had an answer. To me, that confirmed there was no "better" than Nicholas.

*　*　*

Around Halloween, someone had apparently decorated Nicholas' house with toilet paper and pumpkins, but they had written "Nicholas Loves Priscilla" on the toilet paper streamers.

Nicholas called me and said, "I know you did it!"

What? I felt so hurt he would accuse me of such a thing. "No, I didn't!" I pleaded.

"Who else would it be?" He hung up on me before I had the chance to answer, but I called him right back.

"I have nothing to say to you," he said as soon as he picked up. "And I have a girlfriend. Priscilla says I shouldn't have anything to do with you, so I don't want anything to do with you." He hung up again. I didn't call back that time.

A few days later, my sister answered a call on the house phone and shouted to me that it was Nicholas. Despite the fact that my friends had warned me again not to have anything to do with him, I raced toward the phone feeling happy and eager. Maybe he wanted to talk to me after all?

When I picked up the phone, he said, "Okay, I owe you an apology. I know you didn't do it. I found out one of my friends did it."

"Right. Thanks...are we still friends?" I asked, choking up.

"Yes," he said.

I was so happy to hear his voice, and I felt more in love than ever.

Nicholas contacted me one night about a week or so after his apology and took me for a ride in his car. I was so excited to be in his gorgeous car. Maybe he was falling in love with me! Maybe now we'd get somewhere!

He drove us to an empty lot behind an old warehouse, telling me it was okay because he'd been there before. We started fooling around, and then he asked me to give him oral sex. The very idea grossed me out, but it was Nicholas. Plus, I figured I had no choice. It was part of sex, part of growing up. So I just had to get over myself and do it.

I braced myself for the worst-tasting, most vile, disgusting thing I'd ever had to do. To my surprise, and relief, there was no bad taste at all while I did it. But I'd never done it before, so I was thinking I must've done a terrible job.

After a couple of minutes, I stopped, looked up at him, and

asked how I'd done. "Honestly?" he said, grinning. "It's one of the best I ever had." Wow, I felt great. His comment made me feel good. It made me feel like the best.

Nicholas never got round to telling me I was his girlfriend. When he'd had enough, he simply took me home.

Later that week, I was waiting for the bus with Katrina and the hot topic of Nicholas was being discussed in great detail. From over Katrina's shoulder, I saw a student walk out of the little store near the bus stop. I knew she'd fooled around with Nicholas in the past. She spotted me and shouted from several feet away, "Are you going out with Nicholas Valentino?" She stared at me with her mouth wide open.

"I wish" was the first thought that came into my head, but I felt scared. I was so intimidated by this girl. We weren't going out and I wasn't about to lie, so I said, "No." I wanted to come across as somewhat tough and assertive, so I mustered up the courage to ask, "Why?"

Looking relieved by my answer, she turned away to walk back to the store where her friends were. "Nothing, never mind."

Wow. Until that moment, that girl had never uttered so much as a word to me. Yet somehow, she had heard something about me and Nicholas. I was used to such things by that point—people finding out my business even though I'd said nothing to no one about it. There was a part of me that felt proud. I'd been with a guy that a popular girl had been with. I'd officially entered "popular"—like I'd crossed a magical line or something.

Chapter 19

As part of the graduation process, seniors had a Christian retreat to go on in October or November every year. One of the retreats was at a place called Christian Island. There were two trips to Christian Island in October—half the girls went on the first, and half the girls went on the second. Between the two trips, almost all the senior girls would've been on their retreat for the year. Then there was the November retreat, which wasn't as popular as the October one and was only ever attended by a few of the Stella girls.

My parents, perhaps unsurprisingly, strongly recommended I do the November one, saying I'd get more out of it. My parents had done it themselves, so I felt I had to do it too. Regardless of my mixed feelings about the trip, I signed up for it anyway.

In October, Bella, Jordan, India, and Amelia—pretty much all my friends—went on the first trip to Christian Island. Bella kept me up to date by phone and told me about all the funny antics they'd engaged in during the night in each other's rooms. I pictured them in their dark bedrooms, knocking on each other's doors and fooling around. I felt left out. I wished I had gone with them.

Why did I have to go on this other retreat again? Ah, because I was my parents' daughter. I was supposed to. I stood out. I was special. I had obligations. I was "better."

In November, I went on my senior retreat. There were a couple of girls from my year there, but even they were barely acquaintances of mine. The rest of the girls were from other schools and all seemed to know each other. They were nice, but I didn't think they liked me very much. They ignored me for most of the trip.

The retreat was from Thursday evening to Sunday evening. It was held in a high school retreat house. My father used to teach there, but when I was nine, he got fired due to going on strike with other teachers against the school. I remembered being there with him that day.

For a while after he was fired, we severely struggled financially. It was at that time, when I was nine, that my father's temper and violence skyrocketed, including more yelling and more hitting than usual. It was a terrifying time for me. I think that's when I'd felt most vulnerable.

So I was back there again. The retreat house had twin bedrooms so that each student had a roommate. I was incredibly shy during that retreat. I wound up being haunted by feelings from the past—scared, inhibited, insecure, and socially anxious. I felt alone.

We had to get up at the crack of dawn each morning, usually for a mass. I hated getting up early anyway, but I especially resented those early mornings because they were on the weekend. Plus, we usually were up late the night before due to another mass or prayer service we'd had to go to.

Each afternoon, my roommate and I would go to our room to take a nap. We didn't really talk to each other, so it was pretty awkward. However, a couple of days into the retreat, she actually spoke to me across the room from her bed. "Do you feel like all we do is sleep?" she asked.

I felt stupid. Yes, I did, and it was all my fault. I couldn't socialize, and it seemed like she was pointing it out.

I jumped up off my bed and said, "Yeah, you're right."

For the remainder of the afternoon, we actually had many great conversations. As usual, I wound up talking a lot—maybe too much. I'd gone from barely talking at all to not being able to shut up. I told her all about my current life and all about Nicholas. I'm sure she thought I was crazy, and she no doubt pitied me for my many issues. Indeed, I was going after a guy who already had a girlfriend and who was obviously using me. Whenever we were in our bedroom, I'd talk to her nonstop. She couldn't ever get a word in edgewise, which is probably why I don't remember her telling me a single thing about herself or her life.

As the weekend went on, I found myself really wanting to go home. Although a part of me knew the experience was good for me, I felt weird and out of place.

While the priest was talking to the gathering during one of our prayer services, images from my past suddenly came to me. I had flashbacks to my younger years when I was actively involved in the church and feeling close to God. I thought about my birth name, Mary Carol. It hit me that I'd barely thought of God or Jesus in quite some time. I felt guilty, like a sinner who had fallen.

To my utter embarrassment, tears came to my eyes. It wasn't the right time to cry, I thought. I didn't want anyone to see. No one was looking at me, but the priest might see me.

Thankfully, I managed to dry my eyes before anyone noticed. I felt awful about myself, like I was a bad girl, a sinner.

The exact same thing happened during one of our group chats that evening. For the second time that day, I burst into tears when I didn't want to. It was hard not to cry. I was having memories of being shy and not fitting in.

The leader of the group pulled me aside shortly after our group session. "I wanted to talk to you, Mary," she said quietly.

"Why?" I asked.

"I can see you have a lot of pain in your eyes."

Pain? Pain. I'd never considered that I was someone in pain. Hearing it suggested didn't make me feel good. Did that mean I was an unhappy person? Someone who had an unfortunate life? I didn't want to be that kind of person.

I talked to the group leader for quite a long time, telling her about my difficulties socializing with others, feeling shy and scared to approach them. I used the word "insecure" a lot.

Since I'd already opened up to the leader, I then decided to talk to the priest about my feelings.

He talked about a whole host of stuff with me, but what I remember most was when he said, "I can't believe you feel insecure. I thought you'd be the last person to be insecure! I mean, you're attractive, you're intelligent. I never would have guessed you felt that way." It made me feel better to know that I didn't appear insecure. On the outside, I looked like a success. Good.

On the Saturday night, about ten girls and I sat in a small room with the leader to have a rap group. Stronger than ever, I was feeling the "pain"—as I then called it—of insecurity and not fitting in. When it was my turn to talk, I started crying and told everyone how I was feeling about myself. At first, the whole group was silent in response to my confession, but then I got some good feedback from the girls as they slowly started to respond one by one.

The girl on my right said, "I love the way you talk. I could sit here and listen to you talk forever. You're an awesome kid."

I hoped her positive comments would help me overcome my shyness for what was left of the weekend, but one of the teachers in charge later said to me, "If you think you're not going to fit in, you won't."

As cruel as her words were, she was right. The girls remained in their cliques and felt totally unapproachable. I couldn't bring myself to even try to socialize with them.

On Sunday morning, everyone at the retreat met as a group. Apparently, there was a surprise for us. Each of us received letters from people we knew who had already been on the same retreat. I don't know how the retreat people and Stella had pulled this off, but they did.

I got a letter from my parents, which made me cry because they wrote about how proud they were of me and how much they loved me. I also got a couple of other letters from family friends. But the one I will never forget was the letter I got from Ms. Rayfield, my gym teacher.

Ms. Rayfield's letter to me was awesome. She wrote lots of great things about me, complimenting me. She mentioned that she admired my attitude and how I handled people treating me badly. She wrote, *Mary, your goodness, kindness, and love for others shines through. Never lose sight of who you are and why you are you.*

That letter meant a great deal to me and it made me cry—again. I cried so hard I had to put my head down on the table to hide my face. Not that I ever let anyone see, but my nose had also run all over my notebook.

*   *   *

Because Sunday was the last day, everyone's parents were supposed to come for an evening service. The service was nice, but I was happier when the leader announced it was time to go home.

The next morning, Monday, I was on the bus traveling to school. As the bus rode through Howard Beach, I marveled at how refreshed I felt, both mentally and physically. That along with being glad the retreat was over. Finally, I was back to school where I felt more socially confident with all my friends.

Later in November, I discovered that Savannah and Jetta had been talking to a couple of other people about me, saying things like, "She thinks she's so pretty," and "she thinks she's such a good dancer."

When I talked to Bella about it, she said, "They're saying that because both of those things are true...you are pretty and you are a good dancer!" This made me pity the two girls rather than hate them. They resented me, and I suddenly realized how jealous they really were.

Katrina and all my other friends detested Savannah so we often made fun of her, but we also made fun of Jetta and their friend Rose. Rose was a chubby girl, who I thought looked Hawaiian. Apparently, I called her a "fat Hawaiian bitch" behind her back to my friends. I didn't recall having said that about her, but it was brought to my attention one afternoon on the train.

I was sitting on the train along with Savannah, Jetta, and Rose, as well as with Katrina, Dolly, and a freshman we were friendly with, the one who had come with me to see the nuns about Bella's poem.

I noticed that Savannah, Jetta, and Rose would whisper to each other and laugh every time I opened my mouth to talk. Although I was shocked and hurt, I confronted them on it, only to then have all three of them snapping at me and accusing me of talking about them behind their backs.

Rose yelled, "You called me a 'fat Hawaiian bitch.' I know I'm fat, but you shouldn't be saying things like that."

Jetta added, "And you told Savannah you're not best friends with her anymore but you're best friends with Katrina? Well, fine, Rose is best friends with my sister!"

The three of them were right about me on those points, but I didn't feel it excused how nasty they were being or how they were making fun of me. My other friends, though I knew they were on my side, did not come to my rescue. I felt somewhat betrayed.

Knowing the right thing to do was to make peace with Savannah, I took her to another car of the train and started to talk to her. Being her friend wasn't important, but I couldn't have her not liking me! Much to my embarrassment, I started welling up with tears. Savannah looked uncomfortable, like she didn't really want to be there.

Being saved by the train pulling in to my stop, I said goodbye and ran onto the platform. I hated crying in front of anyone.

When I arrived home, I decided I needed to get back at Savannah, Jetta, and Rose. They'd humiliated me, so I had to show them who was boss. I needed to kick some ass. Rose should be the first victim, I thought. She was the one who'd talked Savannah and Jetta into hating me. But, most importantly, I would have help in kicking their ass. Bella, Jordan, India, and Amelia couldn't stand Rose. They didn't like Savannah or Jetta either, even though they were nice to their faces.

I phoned Katrina and told her I wanted to kick Rose's ass. She jumped at the chance to support my plan.

Next, I phoned Jordan. When I told her what had happened on the train, she said, "Oh my God. You know, I had a feeling I should've taken the train with you today. I had this weird feeling something bad was going to happen!" Jordan was also supportive of physically hurting Rose. She said she would call Amelia and India and tell them what was going on.

Last on my list, I called Bella. She, too, was angry and indicated that Rose was in big trouble. She said Rose was going to find out that anyone who had a problem with me, also had a problem with her, Jordan, Amelia, and India.

Having finished my list of calls, I felt comforted, flattered, and just better. I no longer felt like a victim now that I had all these people on my side.

Katrina and I hung out that weekend, which ironically happened to be Thanksgiving weekend, and we talked about how we were going to get Rose. I did most of the talking, Katrina just joined in with me. We also enrolled into our plans a guy named Tim who lived in our neighborhood. I had chatted a lot with Tim before, mainly because he constantly talked to me whenever he saw me.

We brought Tim down to Katrina's basement and told him all about Rose, Savannah, and Jetta and everything that had happened. I was having fun. I wasn't attracted to Tim, but I was in the mood to fool around with someone, just for fun. I had that need to be the conqueror, a female stud.

After going over the details of what we were going to do to Rose, Tim wound up kissing me, right in front of Katrina, too. Poor Katrina quickly excused herself, and he and I went back to his place. He'd already told me his parents weren't home. We went straight to his bedroom and he turned out the lights. As we fooled around on the bed in the dark, I knew in the back of my mind I was making a huge mistake, but another part of me—the female stud part— wanted to do it regardless.

We took off our clothes on his bed, but I left my jeans on. I had my period, so I thought it would be gross if we had sex. Also, I didn't want to have sex with him. That was where I drew the line. I knew that would be a step too far; it would be wrong.

"Can I fuck you?" he asked quietly as he lay on top of me.

I felt cheaper than I ever had in my life, but I didn't want to be seen like a geek by telling him I didn't want to have sex. So I told the half-truth. "No, I have my period," I said.

"Oh, okay," he replied, laughing.

I voluntarily gave him oral sex. I couldn't believe I was doing that; I didn't even like him. After all, he wasn't Nicholas. But, for some reason, I just wanted to. Maybe it was because I wanted to be "bad." When I stopped, he told me to do it again. I didn't want to do it again because I felt I'd done the wrong thing, so I did it with my hands instead. Eventually, he came, and I just wanted to get the hell out of there.

After we'd put our clothes back on, he walked me outside and we stood in front of his house talking for a while. "Do you still respect me?" I asked. I really didn't care if he respected me or not, I just didn't know what else to say. Or maybe I'd asked because I didn't even know if I respected myself.

"Of course," he replied, smiling.

I agreed to meet with him again, even though I knew that was not going to happen. I wasn't attracted to him. That night was just a thing, just fun, just a conquest for me.

By the time Monday morning after Thanksgiving came, me and the girls had our plan together. I'd spoken with Jordan, Amelia, India, and Bella to make sure we were all going to be on the eight o'clock train in the morning, the same one that Rose, Savannah, and Jetta would be on.

So far that year, I'd had perfect attendance with no absences or lateness at all, which was huge for me. I had been planning on continuing that so I'd get a Perfect Attendance Award at the end of the year. However, I decided I'd take the chance of being late to ensure we'd have enough time to kick Rose's ass good.

Katrina and I boarded the eight o'clock train. We saw Dolly standing nearby, along with Jordan, India, and Amelia, all smiling at me. Sitting down was Bella, and next to her on either side was Savannah and Jetta.

Unfortunately, Rose was not on the train. Flooded with disappointment, I explained to India that Rose was not there.

"Aw!" India exclaimed.

Talking loud enough for Savannah and Jetta to hear, the other girls and I discussed over and over how we were going to kick Rose's ass.

Suddenly, Savannah turned to face me. "Don't you dare!" she yelled. "Don't you dare touch my friend!"

Several people laughed at her and imitated her in a squeaky voice, "Don't you touch my friend!"

With the entire crowded train watching, seemingly entertained, I snapped back at Savannah. The comments and cheers the other passengers gave implied they were on my side, especially after I yelled at Savannah about what she and her friends had done to me a few days before.

The more I thought of all the crap I'd gone through with her, how she had hurt me, and how I'd made a promise to everyone and myself that I'd beat someone up, the angrier I became.

Without even thinking, I leaned over Bella's shoulder and slapped Savannah in the face.

The next part was blurry. I couldn't believe I'd slapped her. Savannah and Jetta jumped up from their seats and started yelling at me. In fact, it seemed everyone on the train got up and shouted, my friends included.

India dragged me to the side and held me back from doing any more. But she was smiling. "Stay over here, Mary, just stay here."

"Oh my God, India, I can't believe I just slapped her." I didn't regret it, I just couldn't believe I'd done it.

Katrina came over to stand with India and me while Jordan and Amelia yelled at Savannah and Jetta.

Jetta was shouting, "I'm going to kick her ass! Savannah, she slapped you...I'm going to kick her ass!" I wasn't scared, I knew the others wouldn't let her touch me.

Savannah protested about how I shouldn't be treating her that way, and how I shouldn't have gotten people to gang up on her.

"Well, Savannah," Amelia butted in, "now you know how it feels. It's exactly what you did to Mary the other day!"

Jordan then protested Jetta's constant standing up for Savannah, to which Jetta yelled in reply, "Savannah's my sister! It's only like you lot standing up for Mary!"

"Well then, goddamn it, Mary's my sister!" Jordan shouted, laughing.

Amelia pointed to Jordan saying, "And she's my cousin! So it's a family thing now!"

I called Savannah a racist name, then I heard her and Jetta call me a guinea. Then I heard from someone in the crowd, "Ooh she called you a slut!"

"What?" I yelled.

"You are, Mary, you are!" Savannah started listing guys.

Meanwhile, Dolly was walking around us all and playing an imaginary violin, which Katrina found really funny. Bella, for the most part, stayed in her seat.

"I'm going to kick her ass! I'm going to kick her ass!" Jetta kept saying, pointing at me.

India said, "Jetta, you keep saying that. Why don't you just come over here and do it?"

"I will! I will!"

We laughed when she didn't move from the spot where she was standing.

Someone in the crowd pushed past me to get off the train and said loudly to me about Jetta, "Be careful with her, she's a big girl."

Another person getting off the train said to Jetta and Savannah about me, "She's right. You're wrong."

Tanya, the traitor to black people, was also making fun of

Savannah from a few seats behind us. She shouted to Savannah, "Pipe down, or I'll make fun of your shoes!" That sent us all into hysterics; Savannah wore the corniest, most nerdy shoes with big bows on them.

Jetta asked how I was feeling about slapping Savannah. I responded, "I feel fucking great!" People laughed and cheered.

*　　*　　*

In gym class that morning, the train incident was all my friends and I could talk about. Bella kept talking with admiration about how I'd slapped Savannah. "I'm sitting there, and suddenly, *boom!* Mary slaps her." I kept hearing her shout *"Boom!"* as she described the incident to different people. It was quite strange how much people loved the fact that I'd gotten physically violent with an enemy.

The story spread around to everyone in school like wildfire. A girl who'd often taken the train with Savannah over the years came up to me in the cafeteria and praised me for what I'd done. "I hate her!" the girl said of Savannah.

During the lunch period, Emma had apparently gone up to the cafeteria microphone and said, "Hey, Savannah, how's Mike Tyson?" Supposedly, Savannah said something back and Emma got mad and snapped at her.

Later, Emma and her friend, girls who usually hated me, came up to me excitedly and told me all about the announcement dedicated to me during lunch. I was so happy that these girls were being nice to me, were respecting me, and seemed to admire what I'd done. It was almost too much for me to handle.

In home ec, my friends and I sat at our table sewing the teddy bears we were making, while the other girls sat at another table. Emma was in that class, too.

Bella told the whole story again to everyone at our table. "And then *boom!* Mary leaned over me and slapped her."

"Go, Mary," the girls said. "You should have punched her!"

When Emma came over to our table to hear more, the smile on my face was a mile wide. I wanted her to stay, so I started telling her things about Savannah and how I'd been sick of her. Emma seemed totally on my side about that. All day, for the rest of the day, I went to all my classes on a high.

The next day after school, me and a couple of my friends saw Savannah's mother had come to pick her and Jetta up. We found it hilarious that they'd had to bring Mommy in.

Chapter 20

One night, Katrina and I were at her house. We started playing a silly game of chasing each other from room to room. I closed her bathroom door and pressed my face against the glass so that, as a joke, in her dimly-lit house, my blurry ghost-like face might freak her out.

"Oh my God, Mary," Katrina said, suddenly sounding serious.

I opened the door. "What?"

"That scared me," she said, struggling to catch her breath.

"What scared you?" I laughed.

"*That* really scared me, that face thing you just did." As her bottom lip started to tremble, I saw she really was serious.

I wrapped my arm around her shoulder and tried to comfort her, and she started to explain about her fear of death and how she was scared all the time. At one point, she looked at her cat and for some reason, the way her cat "looked at her" started to freak her out too. It seemed like she was having some sort of breakdown. I got scared. Now it was me who was freaked out. We were alone. The rest I don't remember.

Katrina wrote me a letter saying she needed help and was thinking of seeking counseling. There was something I didn't like about the letter, although I couldn't put my finger on it. Perhaps I was afraid it would take attention away from me if Katrina ended up being the one who needed help. I loved Katrina and I knew she needed help, but her seeking it out was threatening to me.

Feeling depressed and worried, I read her letter again on a cloudy morning on the way to school. I wanted the attention back on me. To my mind, we'd always lived for me, for my life. She'd always been behind me if I had a fight, if I liked a guy, if something happened at home. I had kind of been the one constantly in the spotlight. My spotlight.

This all stirred an emotional reaction in me on the way to school that morning. I decided I wanted help and attention, too, but I didn't know how.

Regardless of my motives, there was something inside me that wanted help. What happened with Katrina just brought it out of me. I was feeling pain similar to that of my childhood.

My emotions built up all day until English class. I sat in the very back of the classroom, near the door.

While everyone else was in the middle of a discussion, tears started coming to my eyes and a lump formed in my throat. A part of me was embarrassed to cry in front of people, but another part of me wanted to cry in front of everyone. And not just for attention. It was so that these girls who disrespected me and made fun of me so much might see a different side of me, instead of the passive stone-like girl I could be when I was being made fun of.

So I let the tears come to my eyes and allowed myself to appear to be on the verge of a breakdown. The teacher took notice of my apparent state and asked me if I was okay. Everyone turned around. Even though my head was turned down, I could feel everyone's eyes staring at me.

When I burst out crying, the room immediately fell silent. "I'm sorry, I'm really out of it today," I said to the class, not looking up. I stood up and walked toward the door. "I have to leave the room."

I left, still crying, and decided to go downstairs to see the school counselor. It felt like the obvious and right thing to do.

I made my way through the maze of deserted halls and stairways and knocked on Ms. O'Hara's door a few minutes later. She took me in and sat me down on a comfy couch next to a box of tissues.

I don't remember much about our session other than thinking how Ms. O'Hara looked like a relatively young counselor. "You look so sad," was the first thing she said in a sympathetic voice. That wasn't helpful; it only made me feel worse.

The rest of that day was a bit of a blur, but I was glad about what I had done.

In home ec the next day, we were busy with our projects when I heard one of my enemies say from the other table, "Mary Powell, next time you leave the room, close the damn door!" Apparently, when I'd left the English classroom crying, I'd left the door open and the poor thing had to get up and close it herself.

Another acquaintance of ours said she'd heard about me crying and wanted to know what was wrong.

I felt on the spot but managed to say, "I...I was just feeling depressed."

"Depressed? What do you have to feel depressed about? You're a pretty girl, you're clever, you're..." She started to list positive qualities about me and life. This was the same girl who had snapped at me and called me "Hitler" when I was in charge of an aerobics routine the year before.

*   *   *

Christmas was coming. My parents, especially my father, were making a big show of the supposed fact that we had virtually no money. For that reason, he was refusing to give me any money so that I could buy presents for my friends.

I was totally embarrassed about this whole situation, especially when I had to tell my friends I couldn't buy them presents that year. They were all understanding, telling me I didn't have to, but it was still humiliating.

I still wanted to do something for my friends for Christmas. They deserved it, and I deserved it too. So I decided to give them each a special gift.

I had so many intense connections with my friends. I loved them so much. Deciding to pour my heart out to them, I wrote them each a letter. For Christmas that year, my gift was to be love and friendship.

It took me hours to write them. But I was also excited about the project because it meant a great deal to me. While writing some of them, I cried.

The last day before Christmas vacation, I handed Bella, Amelia, Jordan, India, Katrina, and Dolly their letters while we were on the train. A few of them read theirs right then and there. A few wanted to save reading theirs for later.

Dolly finished reading hers and said, "Oh, Mary, I love you." At first, I felt uncomfortable with such a genuine expression like that— someone saying they loved me. Amelia read hers, too. In one part, I had written in her letter that I felt she sometimes didn't like me. I also told her how much it meant to me that she'd stood up for me against Savannah.

She put down her letter, sort of laughing, "I've liked you the whole time, Mary!"

With it being our last day, I received Christmas presents from each of my friends. As a joke, Dolly had gotten me a cup that said, "Ho! Ho! Ho!" with a Santa face on it.

Katrina laughed hysterically, saying, "That's perfect for her!"

Part of me enjoyed their comments. Another part felt

uncomfortable. Did they really see me as promiscuous? However affectionate they meant it to be, it was now a label for me. Was this really a good thing? The part of me that loved the attention was powerful and demanding. I decided, again, to keep up the role.

After Christmas break was over, I walked to the front of the cafeteria on our first morning back and saw Bella, Jordan, India, and Amelia sitting together.

As I approached their table, Bella saw me and said from her seat, "I read your letter. *Three* times." This made me feel really good. It gave me a feeling of accomplishment, that I was special, that I had a gift for writing—being honest and expressing my heart to people who mattered to me was something I did well.

*   *   *

Martin had been in my class in junior high. He was a total jerk. One teacher even called him a shithead behind his back in a rap group she led that some of us girls attended.

The only good thing about Martin was that he had this older brother, Randy, who Katrina and I thought was gorgeous. I was definitely interested in him, although I'd never really pursued it.

Randy belonged to a gang called "Fuck the Rest" or "FTR" for short. There were three girls from Stella in it, all of whom were a year behind me. These three girls were often on the buses when Katrina and I were on them, but they made a point of ignoring us. Their behavior was making it quite clear that they saw us as geeks and no one worth socializing with. My typical pattern at Stella, I thought. These nasty, snobby popular girls, when they didn't know me, would be interested in me at first, and then they'd get to know me a little and ditch me as soon as they realized I wasn't like them. I assumed this pattern was because I was uncharismatic, quiet, insecure, shy, and didn't look good. The kind of friends they wanted had quite the opposite qualities.

Anyway, Randy and I became friendly and we would talk on the phone every now and then. I didn't see us being together, but there was a small bit of hope in me that we would, simply because he was cute.

One day, Katrina and I were hanging out in the neighborhood and we ran into Randy. We took a ride with him in his car, with the two of us sitting in the backseat. I was so excited. I was in his car! I was with him! Maybe this would lead to something, I thought.

As we drove by a teenage couple, Randy suddenly yelled, "What are they doing here?" When I asked what he meant, he explained he was referring to the fact that the two were Hispanic. Ours was a white neighborhood, and it was virtually unheard of and unacceptable for non-whites to enter. For many of the people in our neighborhood, ethnic minorities were not "allowed" to ever approach.

His "non-white" attitude turned me off. But not enough for me to not be attracted to him.

One day, one of the people who hung out with this rap gang gave Bella a note for me. Bella handed me the note with a frown on her face as she passed by my locker between classes. She didn't hang around.

The note was folded. On the top of the folded part, my name was written with a big *X* across it. I opened it and read, *Fuck with FTR and see what happens.*

I was freaked out and confused. What had I done to get FTR mad at me? There was a tiny part of me that wasn't surprised. I always seemed to get myself in bad situations with the wrong people. Had I said or done anything to them? I knew what my mouth could be like.

That evening, I decided to call Randy to find out what was going on. He told me what the fuss was about. It had been discovered that my sister had been hanging out with the Hispanic couple we'd seen that time as well as other Hispanic kids.

"And if that's true, then it's all over," he said.

I wasn't sure what he meant by "it's all over." Did it mean that her life was in danger? My life? I loved my sister so much, I didn't want anything bad to happen. I had to beg Randy not to do anything. I had to beg this guy, directly playing to his narcissistic male ego, to prevent anything from happening. I told him that if he were my friend, he would not allow anything to happen.

"So are you my friend?" I asked.

After a long pause, he reluctantly said, "Yeah."

Nothing ever happened. I was so grateful and proud of myself that I'd managed to convince Randy not to do anything. I wasn't totally bullshitting him. I really did feel betrayed by him. It hurt me that he had turned against me. And in asking him "are you my friend?" I wasn't just trying to convince him to not do anything violent, I was also wanting to make him become my friend again, or at least put him back on my side.

*   *   *

I found out that these two girls in my year, ones that certainly didn't like me, had been elected the leaders of the new dance team. The assistant principal in charge of student activities had chosen them. I was a little hurt that I hadn't been chosen. After all, I was involved in more dance-related activities than the two of them put together. I'd been in the Blue and Gold dance team every year—and won, I might add—I was a cheerleader, I was in the hip hop dance team, and I was co-captain of the aerobics team the year before.

Had Danielle, the usual dance leader, been chosen over me, I would have understood. But if she hadn't wanted to do it, then I should have been next.

I had a lot going on related to dance performances. Between the cheerleading routines, the dance team, the hip hop team, and the Blue and Gold's dance and aerobics teams I'd be joining within the next month, I had five performance commitments in total. In addition, I belonged to the liturgy club and had to write morning prayers. Well, strictly speaking, I didn't have to write my own, I just told myself I had to. I also had classes. Fortunately though, I no longer had Regents or any really hard classes to worry about.

I don't know how I managed everything, but I had a ton of energy and my memorization of dance steps and determination were sky-high. So I could "do it all," I told myself. But there were times I got extremely overwhelmed, times when how much I was doing would really hit me.

I relayed my concerns to Katrina in a letter. Letters and notes were very common between the two of us, and between people in my high school in general.

Katrina had replied to my letter with a note, which I opened as I sat down in my seat. She had written sympathetic comments in response to my having told her I was overwhelmed. She started talking about everything she had to do and had written, *Oh man – stress. But hopefully things will die down soon for you.* I loved Katrina knowing about everything I was going through. I wanted her to admire me. She defined me, in a way, and she seemed to have a certain image of me that made her look up to me.

*   *   *

As the end of the school year drew nearer, it was hitting me more and more that soon I'd be leaving Stella. It hurt. As tough as it had been at times, it had been the best four years of my life. Having made a ton of friends, being popular with them and becoming the center of constant attention had made me so happy.

The extracurricular activities and traditions made me happy, too. Stella was where I learned to dance. That alone had boosted my confidence. I'd been a horrible dancer before, so to know I'd disciplined myself to become one of the best dancers in school was an amazing feeling.

Having failed all my classes early on, I'd turned that around and got eighties in junior year, even nineties this year. Of course, I didn't have Regents classes this year and the classes were easier, but whatever.

Not to mention the fact that guys never used to like me, but now I was getting a ton of experience in that area, too. In all of these areas, I had gone from the bottom to the top. I felt sunny, like I was a real accomplishment. I felt successful. I felt genuinely happy.

Chapter 21

When parents came in to Stella one evening so report cards could be distributed, as was the custom for the first trimester, my parents got the chance to meet all my teachers.

I happened to be with my father when he talked to the nun who taught my speed writing class. I knew I was totally acing this class, but it gave me even more confidence in my abilities when she told my father that I would be good "in the business world." That made my heart soar; I couldn't have agreed more strongly with her.

Open-House night was held shortly after the parent-teacher evening. I volunteered to help out and was put in charge of a workshop for parents interested in sending their daughters to Stella. Katrina would be assisting me, and a number of other students, particularly upperclassmen, would be joining in with the evening, too. Having the opportunity to endorse Stella had me feeling excited and happy. I ended up with my own classroom of parents in one of the science labs, and I spent the evening raving about how amazing Stella was with great enthusiasm and a huge smile on my face. Katrina walked behind me at one point and made a kissing noise to imply I was sucking up. Thankfully, everyone saw the funny side and laughed.

Instead of making me feel excited, the thought of graduating and going on to college made me feel depressed and apprehensive. Although going to college was the only way for me to pursue a career as a psychologist, I felt virtually no interest in going. In fact, it was the last thing on my mind, so much so that if it weren't for my parents pushing and persuading and reminding me about it, I might not have even applied on time.

I applied to a few different colleges, but I was told right away by both my guidance counselor and my parents that I might not make it into a four-year college due to my overall grade point average. My freshman and sophomore years had severely affected it. It was suggested that I apply to a two-year school as a backup, so I applied to a community college in addition to the others. My father raved about it, saying that it was an excellent educational facility with great instructors, even though it was only a community college. My parents helped me fill out the applications when they realized I didn't have a clue what I was doing with them.

*   *   *

The annual Stella Christmas show was always held on the last day of classes before Christmas vacation took place. I was in two performances that year, one for the dance team and another for the hip hop team.

The hip hop dance was the one I was most excited about because I'd be able to really show off my best dance skills. Each dancer had a solo part during the dance routine, and we each had to make up our own steps for our part of the show. When each of us took our turn to dance individually, the leader of our team had an idea that she was going to shout through a microphone and get the audience to chant our name as we danced our solo steps.

I was in the front row, which made me feel good because I knew only the better dancers were in the front row. Not only that, I was going to be one of the first to dance on my own.

Having practiced my steps like crazy for weeks beforehand, I waited anxiously for my five-second solo routine to be called. Then I heard Felicia's voice shout over the mic, "Go, Mary!"

The whole audience immediately started to chant, "Go, Mary! Go, Mary!" Leaping to the front of my team, I lapped up my five seconds of fame and danced well. In fact, I danced perfectly.

When it was all over and most people had left the auditorium, I went back to my homeroom with a couple of friends. Overflowing with excitement and pride, each of my friends told me how well I'd done. One of the popular girls even praised me and gave me a big hug as though she couldn't believe it was me, Mary Powell, she'd just seen dancing.

To me, her words of congratulations were like receiving a diamond encrusted trophy. It was an honor. It was an indication that I'd achieved something good. Approval from a popular girl? I'd never gotten that before. Returning home on a high, I thought about how the whole evening, including me, had been a great success.

Blue and Gold practice was fast approaching. Jordan and I had decided we wanted to be captains of dance, which was pretty major considering Danielle had always been dance

captain in the years before. Worst case scenario, we figured we could just be co-captains, like her assistants within the team.

Jordan and I attended the yearly meeting for people who were interested in being captains for Blue and Gold. When we communicated our interest, the assistant principal implied that because Danielle had been captain for the last three years, if someone new wanted to do it, they would be given priority. Danielle and her preferred co-captain looked less than thrilled about the explanation. The assistant principal concluded the meeting by arranging a second meeting for those who wished to be chosen for captains of teams. Absence, she explained, would result in automatic disqualification.

In truth, I didn't feel up to being the head captain of dance. Blue and Gold was a major event at Stella. I knew that virtually everyone wanted Danielle and her friend to be captains. So if Jordan and I were elected, we would most likely be greeted with opposition and hostility. In addition, although Jordan and I were excellent dancers, I knew Danielle was excellent at choreography.

In the end, we told Danielle that we only wanted to be co-captains and help teach dance. A part of me felt like I was selling myself out—not rocking the boat, giving in, trying to please Danielle just so that I wouldn't be persecuted. But I genuinely didn't want to be a head captain and would've been more than honored to be elected as just a co-captain.

So it was decided. Danielle was elected as head captain, and her friend Vicki, Jordan, and I were also in charge alongside her. Together, we headed up the blue team, which consisted of seniors and freshmen. So, with the addition of one of the freshman girls added to the list of people in charge, there were five of us altogether. I was a captain of the Blue and Gold dance team? That was huge.

I was in the cheerleading team that year as well. Our team would be performing at Blue and Gold too, although it was just as a performance for entertainment in between competitions.

*　　*　　*

In the weeks leading up to Blue and Gold, Jordan and I had amazing fun being captains of the dance team. It was one of the highest statuses to have in school, though I don't think it raised our popularity all that much.

There was one time when I was teaching the dance steps that Danielle and Vicki had created to a small group of girls on the dance team. There were a lot of girls in dance, and each of the five captains—myself, Danielle, Vicki, Jordan, and the freshman captain—were each assigned a small group out of the team to teach.

Vicki came over to me and said, in a joking voice, that Danielle had told her, "Mary's teaching the dance wrong." That made me feel stupid, like a phony, like I didn't really know how to dance, let alone teach dance, and I really shouldn't be a dance captain.

Surprisingly, the captains of the cheerleading squad were holding many practice sessions for Blue and Gold. Cheerleaders always did a major dance routine for the annual event, which was one of the main reasons I'd joined them. We were learning a few cheers here and there, but it took a while for them to get started on teaching us a full dance routine.

During Blue and Gold dance practice, I noticed that a few Rockaway girls gave Danielle a hard time. Some mocking comments flew back and forth, and Danielle looked somewhat upset. I couldn't believe what I was seeing. The Rockaway girls weren't anywhere near as popular as Danielle and her friends. I couldn't understand how anyone would even dare be mean to Danielle, one of the most popular girls in the class, least of all if they were from a separate crowd.

I felt bad for her. Vicki didn't do or say anything to the Rockaway girls but did stay by Danielle's side constantly. Although I felt sorry for Danielle, I also saw her misery as a chance to get closer to her and maybe even fit in with her. At the end of practice, I smiled and praised her for doing a good job that day. She thanked me—albeit rather unenthusiastically.

When I later told Caitlin what I'd done, she disapproved, saying I shouldn't have done it because Danielle never would have done the same for me. A part of me knew Caitlin was right, but a bigger part of me disagreed with her. I knew I'd made a lovely gesture that came from a good place. It reminded me I had a good heart, and I was the bigger person.

*　　*　　*

Around the middle of the year, there was increasing tension and conflict in gym class. It involved my group of friends and a handful of the popular girls. This time, however, this group of girls weren't just after me. I didn't know all the details, but Amelia and a few of her friends had somehow wound up on their bad side. Amelia was their main target.

Jordan, who was Hispanic as well as Irish, agreed with me that the main reason they bothered only me and Amelia was because we were the only white girls in our small group. We figured they didn't really have the guts to pick a fight with the Hispanic or black girls. Jordan thought they had a problem with white girls hanging out with non-white girls. If I had been Hispanic or black during those four years of school, I may very well have not been bothered at all.

Jordan was right. Minority girls were picked on infrequently at best, certainly never intensely like I was. Supposedly, Britney Anderson had muttered something nasty about "green cards." There was also the "Martin Luther King" comment, but nothing was ever said to their faces.

I don't remember exactly what happened in gym to start the fights and arguments between us. The girls in that class had always made fun of me, that was nothing new, but now it was toward my whole group of friends too. In a way it was a relief, knowing their picking and teasing wasn't all on me.

One day, Amelia wound up getting into a huge argument with Nicoletta, Isabella's severely hostile best friend; the one who'd told me "most of us don't like you." It was a verbal brawl, happily witnessed by the entire gym.

Sitting on the bleachers at the time, I started to feel angry as I watched Amelia being yelled at. She was my friend. I was very protective of my friends. Deciding I couldn't just sit by and watch, I stormed toward the arguing pair at the other side of the gym. Because gym class had already ended, most of the girls were already in the locker room, out of sight.

As I marched across the gym, I shouted something loudly in protest. They didn't hear me but, unfortunately for me, Britney Anderson and Tanya did. They started to walk toward me, ridiculing and mocking my actions. Britney threw a balled-up piece of paper at me. Being a chicken shit, I backed up as they approached.

It was one more time in my life where, for a moment, I mustered up the courage to assert myself, stand up to oppressors, brace myself to get knocked down, ridiculed, abused, insulted, and punished. Before anything got too out of hand, Ms. Rayfield stormed into the gym and broke up the nasty argument between Amelia and Nicoletta.

But, after school, the drama continued. Me and my crowd left the school building to go home. As we crossed the street from Stella, Nicoletta shouted out behind us, "Amelia! I wanna finish this, don't you?"

Amelia and Nicoletta yelled at each other while two large crowds began to form in front of some houses across the street from Stella. There was the popular girls' crowd, made up of about fifteen or twenty girls, and ours, made up of about ten.

Seeing how outnumbered we were, we started to walk away. Suddenly, water splashed down all over our crowd from somewhere up above. It turned out some guy had thrown down a balloon full of water or urine or something from the second-floor window of his house.

The popular crowd started cheering and applauding the man who'd done it. We later concluded it was because our crowd was Hispanic and black and theirs was white.

"Thank you, sir!" Nicoletta shouted up at him. "It was well worth it!"

As soon as Nicoletta spoke those words, Jordan let loose. "That's it!" she yelled.

As Jordan lunged at their crowd and started yelling even louder, a few of our girls held her back from running at the other group and attacking. They held her tight, but Jordan was struggling to break away, shouting threatening words and quickly slipping out of her jacket.

I couldn't believe what I was seeing. Everyone—their crowd, our crowd—was silent, staring at her. It shut them up. Jordan was one of the calmest, most reserved people in our school. She never fought or argued, and no one, not even these girls, had ever really bothered her. None of them seemed to dislike her.

After the shouting and screaming, we all walked away and tried to calm Jordan down. We walked all the way down the long block toward the subway. A quick glance over my shoulder confirmed the other girls hadn't followed us.

As we neared the end of the block, even though I couldn't see them, I had a weird feeling the group of bitches were still back there somewhere, watching us. It may have been because I felt the need to also be tough, or it may have been that the anger hit me too—or maybe it was a bit of both—but I decided to throw caution to the wind. Turning in the direction of where I thought they might be hiding, I started to scream something about them being Mafia princesses. But, before I could even get a complete sentence out of my mouth, India and a few others laughed, grabbed me, and turned me around to walk in the other direction with them.

The entire train ride home was spent discussing the details of the event and venting about the group of bitches in general. Knowing my friends would all be staying on the train to travel to Brooklyn when I got off, I felt the need to protect myself. I'd have to walk from the train station and wait for a bus, and I'd be alone. Several of the popular girls traveled to that area; I was scared I'd run into some of them.

I don't remember how or when I'd got ahold of it, but I had a long wooden cane with me on the train. Partly because I was scared and partly because it made me feel tough to have a "weapon." I carried that cane with me all the way home. I remember standing alone with this cane in my hand at the bus stop in Ozone Park, probably looking like St. Joseph out of a nativity play.

I stepped off the bus in my neighborhood and started walking down my block toward my house. I was really revved up, angry, but also kind of on a high from all the drama. There was a part of me that liked what happened—the fighting. It made me feel "tough," even though I hadn't done any fighting myself that day. I was fantasizing, with my cane in my hand, about being tough and fighting people who stood in my way or who gave me a problem.

I felt the need to stop at Jodi's house, who lived some doors down from me. I knocked on her door and excitedly relayed to her the events of the day the second she opened it.

By the next day, what had happened had pretty much spread all over our class. Things continued to be tense between our group and theirs, with little incidents and minor arguments happening here and there.

*　　*　　*

Emotions regarding how some of the nasty girls in our class were behaving toward us started to come up. Myself, Bella, Jordan, Amelia, and a friend of theirs, Amy, were talking to Ms. Rayfield after school one day about the troubles we were having with all of them.

As we talked with Ms. Rayfield, she disagreed with me on something, and the pain of the last several years—all the times they'd bothered me, how I was one of those most severely picked on—came bubbling up to the surface. I burst into tears and ran away from the group. A part of me wanted to be dramatic about it, but the tears were real, I couldn't fake-cry.

Just as I got to the stairwell, the girls and Ms. Rayfield caught up with me and stopped me. Amelia grabbed me and held me in a kind hug. It was so interesting that she, who usually wasn't nice to me, was being lovely and caring since I was crying. Amy, too, exclaimed, "Mary, don't worry, if they bother you, we'll kick their asses!"

Chapter 22

One cloudy day in February, Katrina and I were hanging out outside the mall, waiting for the bus. As we chatted, we both noticed an unbelievably gorgeous white sports car making a U-turn nearby.

This car was unlike anything I'd ever seen before. I can't even describe it. It was out of this world. I decided I had to meet whatever guy was behind the wheel—purely because of his car.

Katrina and I approached his car with excitement. When he rolled down his window, he and I started talking and we eventually exchanged phone numbers. I didn't find the guy attractive at all. He was twenty-four, which seemed really old because I was only seventeen, and he was dark, foreign, which really wasn't my type. But because he had this amazing car, I had to date him. Well, I didn't actually want him to be my boyfriend. What I wanted was for him to pick me up every day from school so all the girls in school could see the car I'd be getting a ride in.

He and I spoke on the phone and set up a date for dinner and a movie. I remember him saying emphatically to me, "Oh, and don't bring any money with you. I'm paying for everything." I realized then that I'd never been on a real date before, not where a guy took me out. Vinnie and I just hung out, so that couldn't be counted as a proper date, and there was that one time I went to a movie with my other ex, Craig, but he didn't want to be there and neither did I, so I didn't count that either.

It was a little scary, especially since he was so much older. I knew I was a bit too young for a man to be taking me to dinner and a movie.

His name was Henry. He came to my house to pick me up, late afternoon, early evening time. My parents had insisted they meet him, so he came inside my house and made himself at home on one of the couches in the living room. As he talked quietly and briefly to my parents, I noticed his clothing—well, his pants and shoes mainly. He was wearing, like, actual men's clothing! Eeew, was my inner reaction. He didn't dress like guys I usually hung around with. He wore slacks and men's shoes, whereas the others had all worn jeans and sneakers.

As I figured it would be, everything felt so weird over dinner, talking to him, and then being in the movie theater with him afterwards. I spent the whole date asking myself what I was doing. I wasn't attracted to him at all and I knew I was just wasting my time. But he had a great car, so I decided I'd date him a little longer.

After a couple more dates with Henry, I didn't bother calling him again. We never even kissed; to me, he seemed way too gross to do anything beyond driving around in his beautiful car.

*   *   *

I was starting to notice that Katrina seemed to be a little less attached to me than normal. While she still had to take the first two buses to school with me, she didn't then join me on the train. Instead, she would take the third bus to Stella with some friends she knew, including some guys from the public school. I occasionally joined her on the third bus, but most of the time I wanted to be with Bella, Jordan, India, and Amelia on the train. We always had such a fun, wild time and I didn't want to miss out.

It was a loss, a void, not having Katrina there. It had previously felt like she'd been all mine, kind of like an attachment, so it was strange seeing her living her own separate life, away from me. Of course, I knew she had every right to, but emotionally, it didn't sit well with me.

I found myself, as usual, feeling I had to prove myself to Katrina—to keep up a tough image, some sort of image that would keep her admiring me. However, my usual tactics no longer seemed to be working. I felt she was slipping away from me. In reality, perhaps she wasn't actually abandoning me—maybe that was just my imagination—but rather she wasn't always making the effort to have me as the most important friend in the world. I was being unreasonable, but I still felt threatened by her having a separate life.

I was bothered by the fact that Katrina's focus seemed to be elsewhere, on others. But, to be fair, mine was too. I was becoming increasingly attached to Bella; I wanted her to be my best friend and I wanted to be hers.

Our distancing was becoming so apparent that Katrina and I were starting to come into conflict. We weren't fighting or even arguing, but she did point out that I would tell her what to do as though she were a child. She implied I was judgmental and said that when she told me about her problems, I gave too much advice. I knew there was some truth to that. I felt the need to control Katrina, and I believed I had all the right answers when younger people told me about their problems.

Katrina said, in one of her letters, *A lot of times it's not what you say but the way you say it.* I knew she was right. I would say certain things to control her, things that had an indirect message. She also wrote, *Sometimes I feel like when you say things about other people, somehow you are talking about me, too*. She was right there, also. If I had negative feelings toward her that I couldn't express directly, I would talk about other people and say negative things about them, which silently included her. Caught!

Katrina and I were drifting apart. I could feel it. What frustrated me the most was that I couldn't put a finger on what was going on. I did know that she was spending less time with me and more time with Missy and others in her year. Often, however, the hostility had some reason behind it—a response to being treated with jealousy or abandonment, like it was a competition. I didn't experience this with all my friends. She was pretty much the only one who gave me that feedback.

Meanwhile, Bella and I were getting closer, but that was more my doing than hers. I was becoming addicted to and obsessed with her—I was always addicted to someone—male or female.

*   *   *

When that year's cheerleading started, it wound up not being as much fun as I thought it would. There were a lot of basketball games, which meant a lot of staying behind after school to learn and perform new cheers for the games. Like the last time I was a cheerleader, I didn't care about the sport or the team, and I still never watched the games.

The only reason I ever had fun in cheerleading was because Jordan was there. Once, we were on the stage in the gym, dancing as the team played, and Jordan messed up one of the cheers. Her mistake was obvious to everyone. She started to laugh and ran off the stage, which I found hysterical. I continued to cheer but struggled due to how much I was laughing. The both of us got a slap on the wrist for that.

I wasn't the neatest person in the world. One afternoon, my cheerleading uniform was so scrunched up, I'm pretty sure the wrinkles could've been seen from the other end of the gym. Bella, India, and Amelia watched while my team and I practiced. "Mary! You're wrinkled!" shouted Amelia, causing the rest of them to laugh. I was embarrassed, so I later explained I hadn't had time to iron my uniform.

"Just throw it in the dryer!" one of them said. I didn't know you could throw a wrinkled piece of clothing in the dryer to get the wrinkles out. Those were things I should have known but didn't. My family was sloppy, I figured, that was why.

*　　*　　*

Although much of the bullying had decreased, I still found myself on the receiving end of some hostility. I overheard one of the girls in my class say loudly to another, "We're going to a game because my friends are cheerleaders." And then she added, "*Real* cheerleaders." They knew I was a cheerleader and made sure to say it loud enough so I could hear. Admittedly, they struck a small chord because I knew that the cheerleading squad wasn't doing a whole lot of good.

Two days before Blue and Gold, the head cheerleaders decided to cram in a dance, in addition to the cheers we'd already prepared for Blue and Gold. I hated having to stay after school to practice. It always gave me a sick feeling. Nevertheless, we managed to learn and perfect a new dance.

The first day we stayed after school was for the dress rehearsal for Blue and Gold. All the teams performed, beginning with the introduction, then art, aerobics, dance, gymnastics, races, and then cheerleading last.

After we cheerleaders had done our bit, just the cheers, not the new dance, we started off to the sidelines to sit back down. As I got to my seat, a bunch of girls on the blue team yelled, "That's it?"

"Mary! Mary!" one of them called.

I turned to see several girls staring at me. "That's it?" they repeated. Unbelievably, especially given that I wasn't one of the captains, they saw me as the easiest target to take things out on.

That same afternoon, after all the other teams had left, us cheerleaders stayed behind to practice our dance. We went home late in the afternoon, only to then have to go back at 8 p.m.

This was to be my last Blue and Gold. The theme was "Blue and Gold Around the World."

The two nights went well. We won dance for the fourth year in a row—from the beginning of high school to the end of high school. Our aerobics team lost, probably because the routine was nothing special—I found it boring. Just regular exercising. The gold team's routine was much better than ours.

The only downside to Blue and Gold was the bitch girls yelling my name during the cheerleading routine. Our dance was really cute, but it was short, which ended up being a good thing because it meant they couldn't shout at me for too long.

When Blue and Gold was over, Jordan, India, and I were going crazy. Later, it turned out a photo of the three of us and Katrina had been taken at that exact moment. It was a terrible photo of me and I hated looking at it—I looked too hyper, almost manic. Katrina had her arm around me, probably to stop me from falling over mid-cheer. The worst part about that photo was my obvious sideburns, which were on display only because my hair had been in a ponytail for the cheerleading routine. The ponytail was also a little too high up, so it looked more like a horse's tail than my hair.

I found out from a guy I knew that Katrina had said, "Mary? She screws every guy she goes with."

I was so done with Katrina. In shock, I called Bella, feeling the need to be tough with anyone who messed with me.

When I asked Bella if I should do something to Katrina, she said, "Kick her ass!"

So I hung up, put on my shoes, left my house, and walked around the corner feeling like some sort of gangster.

Katrina came to the door as soon as I rang the bell. Barely looking at her, I silently gestured for her to come with me. We started walking and I told her what I'd heard. She denied it, of course, but I didn't believe her. Admittedly, even if it wasn't true, I still wanted to hurt her for abandoning me and getting close to Missy.

When we got to the avenue, I started yelling at her. "And Missy is a prissy bitch!"

At that, Katrina's face filled with hurt and anger. "Shut the fuck up!"

"YOU shut the fuck up!" Feeling like I needed to hurt her physically, I charged at her. Really, I didn't know what I was doing.

As I pushed her to the wall of the building next to us, she yelled, "What the fuck!"

Satisfied with my work, I turned and marched away from her, cursing her out as I walked across the street to head home.

"I love you too!" she yelled. She sounded hurt.

In a letter, she later admitted what she said about me screwing everyone was true and apologized. But I knew that our friendship would probably gradually fade. I knew I was wrong to have hit Katrina. I had behaved exactly like my father. And I had chosen, once again, a safe target to bully.

*   *   *

To save up for prom, as my parents were not giving me any

money for it, I'd gotten a part-time job as a telemarketer through a friend of a friend. Less than a week after I started, our office moved, and it was kind of a pain to get to the new one. I had to walk a good mile to get there and again on the way home. I would usually come home from school so exhausted I would need to take a nap, typically for about an hour. When it was time for me to get up and go to work, I was always so sleepy and reluctant to even move. But my father would virtually force me to work, refusing to fully support me financially unless I continued with my job. It was a real drag and a daily dread of mine to know I'd have to be at work by 7 p.m.

Once in work, however, there were people there that I knew and liked. There was one particular girl, Kel, that I'd become friendly with. She was skinny and had weird acne, which I always thought was so gross. There was another girl, Bea, an acquaintance of Kel, who constantly talked about this boyfriend she'd had a lot of drama with—breaking up with him one minute and loving him the next.

Kel once said about it, "Bea screws him every time she sees him."

Wow, I thought as that same feeling came over me, the one I'd get every time I heard about a girl my age having sex. I mean, by that time, I'd had sex too! Well, kind of. But I was still fascinated by this, and I constantly wanted to know if girls around me were having sex. Some weren't, which made me feel special, and some were, which made me feel I had some catching up to do—like they were more mature than me or miles ahead of me in some way.

Though I was still haunted by my social anxiety, I was slowly getting better at socializing. I developed my own little way of doing it. I was somewhat defensive and guarded—I'd be narcissistic and say funny things to be a clown, which made people at work like me—but I never let them get too close. I had to remain in control.

There was an amazingly cute guy there, too. I still didn't have a prom date and spent most of my evening shifts fantasizing about asking him to come to my prom with me. I also fantasized about him being my boyfriend. He often flirted with me, mildly, and socialized with me in his charming, charismatic, and funny way. I found out he had a girlfriend, but that didn't faze me, I just considered it to be an "obstacle" to overcome. I would still go for it if he went for me.

Eventually, I decided to ask him to go. It turned out that "as much as he wanted to go with me," he couldn't "because his girlfriend would kill him." That was understandable, of course, but not to me.

Feeling anxious, I knew his rejection meant I had yet to find a prom date. Bella was hooking us up with limos through someone she knew who could get us a good deal. Of the two limos she planned to organize, one would carry me, Dolly, Mellie, Liz, and our dates, while the other would carry Bella, Jordan, India, Amelia, another friend of theirs, and their dates.

As I wracked my brain for other potential dates, I thought about another guy, Matt, from work, who I thought looked like Matthew Broderick. He was really cute. When one of my co-workers suggested I ask him to the prom, I did. And, much to my surprise, he agreed. I couldn't believe how last minute it was or how easily I'd gotten a prom date after asking him only once.

*　　*　　*

Senior luncheon was at a nice country club. Unfortunately, I had practically nothing to wear since I'd never gotten around to looking at new dresses to buy. I ended up choosing the white dress I'd worn to Ring Day the year before. It was a little embarrassing to have to wear the same dress twice, and I wondered if people would notice or speak negatively of it if they did. Perhaps they wouldn't remember. But the girls at Stella could always be counted on. Britney Anderson noticed it before the luncheon had even started, and there was still about half the class yet to arrive.

I passed a table where Savannah and some other girls sat when Britney Anderson yelled across the room, "Nice dress, Mary Powell."

As usual, I stopped dead in my tracks, became scared, and searched for something to say.

"It is a nice dress. That's why I wore it," I retorted.

"That's why you wore it twice," she said loudly and walked away.

Savannah had been sitting at the table, and I knew that she was smirking, loving it.

I sat with a bunch of my friends at the luncheon table. As joyous as this occasion was, I felt so weird about school coming to an end. I was still obsessed with Bella, so I was a little disappointed by the brief note she left when signing my yearbook. I wanted so much from her; a long note, saying how much I meant to her and that she loved me. Her note was nowhere near as long as mine, but I'd wait and wait for more signs of devotion if I had to.

During the luncheon, Danielle made mention in a speech about how we'd won Blue and Gold dance all four years of high school. The clean sweep still seemed pretty amazing to me. As much as I didn't like Danielle, I knew she was responsible for us winning.

At the end of the luncheon, when everyone cleared out to go home, Dolly grabbed ahold of one of the huge plants that were displayed as centerpieces on each table and walked right out with it. A few of us followed her, laughing hysterically as she struggled to balance in her heels under the weight of the heavy clay plant pot.

One of the nuns saw Dolly and shouted, "What are you doing? Put that back!"

"Oh, but, sister," Dolly said, looking at the gigantic plant in her arms and then back at the nun. "I thought we were supposed to take one." Several of us had tears in our eyes by that point through laughing so much.

Her mouth gaping open, she stared at Dolly and then at me in disbelief. "You are crazy! You are absolutely crazy!"

I was somewhat embarrassed by the fact that this woman now thought I was "crazy." I was also a little envious of Dolly. Even if I'd wanted to, I couldn't make such witty jokes like that, and the couple of girls around who laughed at Dolly's antics would never have laughed if I'd done what she did. I still saw myself as an outcast.

Chapter 23

I was working on the day before prom, which really sucked because it was a sunny, beautiful day and I could've thought of far better things to be doing. During my lunch break, I did something I'd never done before and went to get my nails done. I wanted tips that were a French manicure, and they turned out looking absolutely gorgeous.

That night, I called Mellie to tell her all about my new nails, but as soon as she got on the phone, she screamed at me about how excited she was about prom. That's when it hit me how huge this really was. Prom! I'd waited to have a real prom for such a long time.

The next day, I got my hair done in the afternoon and then went home and made a start on getting myself ready. I looked gorgeous in my blue dress; well, at least Bella and her family said I did. I'd felt some slight hesitation about it at first because it wasn't how I'd originally imagined my prom dress to be. I'd imagined something long and flowing, Cinderella-like. But I'd come to accept the painful truth that I just wasn't as good at picking out clothes as most women seemed to be.

Dressing myself up and taking care of my appearance had never been my strong point. It was something I'd always been ashamed of, but it wasn't helped by the many people who cruelly reminded me about it on a daily basis, sometimes in an abusive and malicious way.

The fact that it was a tight dress not only heightened my shame and self-consciousness but also reminded me, once again, that I had a "great figure" and that I "had to show it off." I was the only one of my friends who had that kind of figure. If anything, I found it embarrassing and pressurizing. If I didn't dress a certain way, I wasn't "living up to my potential," but if I dressed the other way—the appropriate way— I was "wasting my potential" by "not showing it off." Either way, I couldn't win.

Bella had taken care of organizing the limo, which was scheduled to start arriving at people's houses at five o'clock. It was to pick up Mellie and Liz—the one who'd lost my English textbook—and their dates at their homes, then Dolly and her date—Amelia's brother— at her home, then me and my date.

Matt looked great in his tux. He'd gotten me a beautiful corsage, and he had a blue cumberbun to match my dress.

I was so happy when he arrived. He met my parents and we all hung out for a while. The limo was supposed to arrive at my house by about six so that we would get to the prom at around seven.

Six o'clock came and went. At about six-thirty, I began to get nervous and contacted the limo company, who said they hadn't been paid enough and were stuck in Brooklyn near Mellie and Liz's.

Freaked out, scared, and in a crazy state of panic, I called Bella to tell her what was going on in the hopes of getting reassurance that the limo would get to us on time.

Bella immediately became angry at the company and said, "Tell those people that we had an agreement to pay them when they got to our houses...they know that!"

I contacted the limo company to relay the angry message from Bella. They gave me a hard time each frantic time I called and kept saying they were on their way. Time passed. And passed. I was yelling, on the verge of tears, and poor Matt was there to witness the whole meltdown, as were my parents. I really didn't care about Matt being turned off or anything, I wasn't that attracted to him and didn't want him as a boyfriend.

When I called again, still yelling, they said the limo was two towns over, still about fifteen minutes away from us. My father offered to drive us to the limo, which the company agreed was a good idea and said the limo would wait where it was.

By this point, it was well past seven, the time the prom was starting. I was so angry and disappointed. Not only was the limo not coming to pick us up from my home, which was something I'd really looked forward to, but we were also now going to be more than fashionably late to the prom.

My mother took Polaroid photos of Matt and me before we left. When I looked at one of the photos, I could see the disappointed "oh well" expression on my face.

My father drove the two of us beneath an overpass off the road, where we immediately spotted the long white limo waiting in all its splendor.

I couldn't believe I was going to be riding in a limo, but the happiness I was supposed to feel was mixed with frustration, disappointment, and negativity.

So, Mellie and her date, Liz and her date, and Matt and I rode in the limo to pick up Dolly and her date, Amelia's brother.

Dolly had brought with her some alcohol—Vermouth wine and Sex on the Beach—which we started drinking in the limo as it drove. Even though I'd sworn a year and a half before to never drink again, I downed my first glass of wine almost in one gulp. I really surprised myself. It felt like I was drinking like a robot, just doing it without any thoughts or feelings.

We had to convince the driver to stop a couple of times along the way so a few of us, myself included, could go to the bathroom.

Once was at a gas station, the other was on the edge of a forest. At the gas station stop, I actually peed in front of my friends. That was super weird, but they were too busy talking to take any notice.

The limo finally pulled up outside the prom location. To my horror, I began to involuntarily sob, just like I had a couple of years before when I'd gotten drunk.

Dolly started hugging me and one of the guys said, "Oh come on, Mary, don't cry."

The rest of the guys started cheering at me, "Mary! Mary! Mary!"

Dolly took me into the bathroom as soon as we got inside. I was so drunk I couldn't make anything out. We went into one of the stalls. I was crying hysterically and, for some reason that none of us could figure out, I kept repeating "I'm sorry, I'm sorry, I feel so bad" to them.

Someone asked me, "Do you want me to go get Bella?" They must have known how attached I was to Bella. Feeling glad that she might come to my aid, I told them yes.

A few minutes later, Bella and Amelia entered the bathroom and Amelia rushed over to me, yelling at me to "stop crying." At one point, she slapped me in the face. I didn't feel any pain, I was too drunk, nor did I really think anything of it. She implied that she was trying to "snap me out of it," but I think she'd done it because she was also irritated by my crying.

I kept saying "I'm sorry, I'm sorry" and crying even more. As we made our way out of the stall, I saw a blurry Britney Anderson staring at me.

I guess she'd recognized that I was drunk because she said to me, "Be careful, you're going to get in trouble!" The girls later told me that I'd responded by laughing in her face. Since when was this bully concerned for my welfare? That's probably why I'd laughed.

Bella and Amelia sat me down at a table, by which time the whole class had arrived, and most people were dancing. My vision was so blurry that I didn't even notice my surroundings. All I knew was that there were a few of my classmates and friends crowding me as I sat and sobbed.

I cried in various people's arms for a while but then finally came out of it. My vision became less blurry, and I noticed that nearly my whole class and their dates were dancing. Matt and I got up and joined in.

When the theme song that had been chosen for our prom was played, I became so excited by the idea that "our song" was playing. It had a special meaning for me. It marked the end of the best four years of my life; it meant I was leaving Stella, and it reminded me that it was my prom. At the end of the song, Matt kissed me on the cheek.

He and I kept slow dancing until we were the only ones left on the dance floor. We didn't, or I didn't, notice that the dance floor had been cleared because they were about to announce the queen of the prom. As we danced, blissfully unaware, a girl yelled, "Mary! Get off!"

I felt like the verbal attack I got this time was more "respectful" and not as humiliating. I wondered if the change was due to them seeing me with a cute guy and because I looked so great. There really wasn't anything to make fun of.

Sr. Agatha, our principal, picked the name out of an envelope and looked at the piece of paper. She looked happy for a moment, even sentimental, and then she announced the queen of the prom as Debbie Pinter.

Some of the girls in my class cheered.

What? Her? She's a bitch and she's not even pretty, I thought.

We had missed half the prom due to being so late, so all that was left was about two hours of dancing time. My blurry, drunk vision gazed around the darkened room we were in, which I saw was decorated with pretty bows and ribbons, and gorgeous chandeliers hung from various points across the ceiling. It seemed smaller than I figured it would be.

I was disappointed, and I felt strange. I hadn't gotten to experience my entire prom. We hadn't even had any photos taken outside in the early evening. Not to mention the fact that I'd arrived drunk and crying so I'd missed even more.

The prom ended around midnight, and I did the best I could to cheer myself up as I stood in the building's entrance waiting for some of my friends. I kept telling myself there was more to come; it was my prom night, which meant I'd be out all night for the first time in my life. I'd never been allowed to stay out so late before.

We all ended up at this pretty restaurant that doubled up as a club. I don't remember much about it since I was still somewhat drunk, though I was in a happier mood by that time and the depression and crying had stopped. Jordan, India, Amelia, Matt and I were dancing on a small, private dance floor. Someone in our group took pictures of us while we danced.

We then went to a diner for breakfast, even though it was still dark outside, and I ordered pancakes. Matt ordered a bran muffin and tea. When he went to the bathroom, my so-called friends started laughing and making fun of him. "Who orders a *bran muffin with tea*?" one of them said. They kept laughing and making jokes, particularly Dolly.

I felt confused. I genuinely thought I'd picked a great guy to go to the prom with, yet they were laughing at him. Maybe my judgment was off, I thought. Maybe, once again, my peers were right. They were always right about behavior, looks, clothes and whatever else. I was rarely right and rarely taken seriously.

After breakfast, our limo drove everyone back home. I was the last to be dropped off, so I spent my alone time pretending I was rich and famous and that was why I was riding in a limo.

Considering how many hours I'd worked to save up enough money for the prom, I was delighted to find I'd spent very little money and still had about two hundred dollars left. I marveled at the stack of unspent notes inside the blue pocketbook I'd gotten to match my prom dress and shoes. As another welcome leftover from the prom, I still had great-looking nails.

I was disappointed that it was over. I think the disappointment was worsened because I'd only really gotten half a prom, and even that was mostly spent being drunk or upset, or both.

Classes had officially ended. I was beginning to feel dread and emptiness because high school, Stella, was coming to a close. With graduation rehearsal and the graduation ceremony being the only part of school left to complete, I tried to focus on looking forward to those.

Chapter 24

The ceremony and rehearsal were going to be held at the public high school near us because our own auditorium wasn't really big enough. I got to the rehearsal somewhat late to find the other students already lined up in the hallway outside the auditorium.

I was fully expecting the girls in line to laugh at me or harass me since I was the latecomer and the automatic center of attention. However, no one did. I was surprised that no one was teasing me, but I guessed they took my drunken stupidity as a sign that I wasn't such a geek after all. Plus, being seen with a cute date didn't hurt.

Caitlin gave me a card for graduation. The outside of the card read, *After all the hassle...* with Ziggy furiously studying, and on the inside, *You've finally earned your tassle!* I stared at the front of the card. It was weird; I hadn't done the hassled, stressed-out kind of studying that was expected. To me, high school had been about friendship and extracurricular activities. I felt guilt, like I'd gotten over somehow.

Knowing what graduation symbolized, I found the practice ceremony difficult to attend and sit through. After today, I only had one more day of Stella left before the graduation ceremony tomorrow, and then it would all be over.

I'd bought two beautiful dresses lately: my prom dress and a dress for graduation. I'd chosen a tight white dress for the ceremony. Interestingly, that was the color I'd chosen for my eighth-grade graduation ceremony, but that previous one was more lacy and showed off more of my skinny body. I'd been called an "Ethiopian" by one of my non-admiring classmates.

Graduation day was a gray, cloudy day. My mood was kind of the same, though I couldn't label the mood as depression at that special moment of my life. Although Katrina was coming to the ceremony, she didn't seem very excited or happy about it and I felt more distanced from her than ever before. I felt so hurt by this, but I couldn't be sure whether or not part of it was just my imagination.

The public school's auditorium was huge and dimly lit. It bore no resemblance to Stella at all and felt fake somehow. We should've had our graduation ceremony in Stella's auditorium, no matter how not fancy it was. It would've been more real, more symbolic—I would've had more of a sense of closure.

Not only was the auditorium dark, it was also humid, so my hair was frizzy and sticking to my neck. The ceremony was kind of boring; I paid attention to nothing except the graduation march, receiving my diploma, and most of all the valedictorian's speech.

The valedictorian had always completely ignored me. Based on the times I'd sat at her table during freshman year, she usually engaged in arrogant, cynical intellectual discussion or gossip. I thought she was a snob and a bitch. And I was jealous. I'd wanted to be valedictorian, but I'd come nowhere near close to achieving that. It was yet another reminder that I wasn't that smart or academically disciplined. And everyone else thought so, too. That could never be me. She and other students were superior to me that way. In comparison, I was a failure, a misbehaved, looked-down-upon, shamed child. All fingers pointed downward at me.

She ended her speech with, "I love you all." Not true. Not all of us. Only the girls she deemed worthy. Not us "scum"—me and my friends.

She was someone I could not be. A reminder that I wasn't good enough compared to these girls—that I had so many defects that, of course, should be teased—which was why I had never fought back.

I got my diploma and a rose. No one loudly cheered for me, but no one snickered at me either. It felt like a somber, distant occasion, and everyone seemed to be a little quiet.

But the happy, crazy, hyper side of me came out after the ceremony. After all, we had just graduated, and I knew this was a big deal; the day I'd been waiting for—both with happiness and sadness—for a long time.

Katrina, always the photographer, snapped pictures of me and my friends, as did my parents. Dolly and I climbed a concrete mount, cheering and jumping. My mom got one of me holding up my graduation cap. I was smiling and enthusiastic looking, but deep down I wasn't thrilled. I didn't want it to be over, especially not like this.

There were plans for all of us to celebrate at Dolly's house later that night. So at least it wasn't over just yet. I had this in mind as I sat in the back of my father's car and we drove down the boulevard. I had that yucky, numb feeling—not happy, not sad. But the depression and disappointment were lurking down there somewhere. I felt like a sudden death had happened in the family, or a wedding day where the ceremony was nice but not what you'd dreamed of your whole life. What was being celebrated made me happy, of course, but something wasn't quite right. Really, my overwhelming emotion was disappointment.

My feelings, I thought, were valid. The celebration of the end of high school for me *was* disappointing. That lousy ceremony, my prom, feeling I was losing Katrina.

High school had been, up to that point, the happiest years of my life, so even the most disappointing of endings in the world wouldn't have canceled that out.

*   *   *

Chapter 25

During senior year, there had been a mass in the school auditorium. On the printed paper booklet, there was a statement that read, *If someone has done the best she could, was enthusiastic and used her talents, then that person has led a full life.*

I felt wonderful and happy reading that. I knew the poem applied to me and my life, especially up to that point! I felt so good about myself—I was a success. I had a ton of friends, which was something I'd never had before I entered high school. I had learned to dance really well, another thing I'd never had before high school. I had been able to let loose and be really loud and fun with my friends, yet another thing I'd not had the opportunity to do before high school.

Academically, I had started my first half of high school doing worse than poor, but I had risen above it and my grades had improved beyond belief.

By this point, my hair looked great and my figure looked more amazing than ever. I looked gorgeous, and I received compliment after compliment from guys, girls, and adults alike—also something I'd never had before.

These realizations are only coming to me as I write this now. I can see that it's little wonder why, when I graduated, I saw the past four years as the best of my life. While one would think, understandably, that I was miserable in school, I was actually very sad and scared to leave Stella. I'd never grown that much in my entire life.

My mother had told me before I entered Stella that going to an all-girls would help me "find myself as girl." Upon beginning this book, I focused mostly on the traumas, abuse, and sexism that occurred in this institution.

I thought that I hadn't really found myself as a girl when I thought back to Stella. But, closing this story, remembering the happy times I experienced while in Stella, I realize that, while the journey was far from over, being at Stella and learning to deal with everything that went on there, everything that happened to me, I had found myself as a girl. I do know it was a huge contribution to me finding myself as a woman—how could it not be? I had risen above the sexism and abuse and achieved in spite of it all.

Even if the environment and Catholic beliefs were dysfunctional at times, on reflection, I realize you can't help but learn about yourself in a student body composed completely of your own gender.

A female who has survived abusive sexism sustains her True Self. My personality, spirit, and behaviors were not altered by the relentless victimization. I felt that sadly, the souls of some of my classmates were.

As opposed to when I began this book, I am no longer experiencing the anger and resentment toward the young women who were so abusive and who I felt overpowered me. My friends and other classmates were right to inhibit ourselves just to survive.

In truth, these popular girls were miserable and in excruciating pain. They had lost their True Selves. Their anger, their bullying—a kind I'd never seen in my life, even amongst the cruelest kids I'd come across beforehand—was a reflection of their hurt, their families. Now, I feel sad and sorry for them rather than hate or fear. I hope and pray that love will save them and that they will heal. They deserve it no less than I do.

References

Greene, M.B. (2006). Bullying in Schools: A Plea for Measure of Human Rights. *Journal of Social Issues.* *(62)*1, 63-79.

About the Author

Dr. Mary Powell, PhD, LCSW-R, NCPsyA, is a psychotherapist and adjunct professor. She has treated numerous adults, adolescents, children, families, and groups in psychoanalytic and dialectical behavior therapy (DBT) for twenty years in both private and public practice. Dr. Powell has presented at several professional conferences on the importance of self-care in clinicians, DBT, and mindfulness in social work education. She received a Certificate of Appreciation for Outstanding Contribution to Social Work Education and a Certificate of Achievement in recognition of Clinical Excellence in the Field of Social Work. Her doctoral dissertation received the Reverend Doctor Langenfeld Award for the Most Outstanding PhD Dissertation. Through extensive personal psychotherapy and her professional work, she has been able to conquer the effects of bullying in youth, a phenomenon that is in need of attention and intervention.